Facing Shame

FAMILIES IN RECOVERY

Merle A. Fossum
Marilyn J. Mason

Family Therapy Institute
St. Paul, Minnesota

W · W · NORTON & COMPANY

New York   *London*

Quote from "Will and Anxiety," from Leslie H. Farber, *The Ways of The World: Essays Toward a Psychology and Psychopathology of Will*, New York: Basic Books, 1966. Copyright © 1966 Leslie H. Farber. Reprinted by permission.

Printed in the United States of America.

First published as a Norton paperback 1989.

Library of Congress Cataloging-in-Publication Data

Fossum, Merle A.
  Facing shame.

  Bibliography: p.
  Includes index.
  1. Shame.   2. Family psychotherapy.
  I. Mason, Marilyn J.   II. Title.
  BF575.S45F67   1986   616.89′156   85-31011

ISBN 0-393-30581-3

W. W. Norton & Company, Inc., 500 Fifth Avenue, New York, N.Y. 10110
W. W. Norton & Company Ltd., 37 Great Russell Street, London WC1B 3NU

  2 3 4 5 6 7 8 9

We dedicate this book to our children – Jeanine, Jerry, Thyra, and Linnea – that they may find courage in facing the dragons they meet, and to our clients – our teachers who went with us in facing shame.

CONTENTS

FOREWORD

The findings of the social scientist followed slowly and long after the insightful perceptions of the poet and the novelist. Research into the intrapsychic world of the individual began with the psychoanalytic work with dreams, parallel with early psychological testing. This soon advanced to the study of interpersonal relationships and was illuminated by learnings from couples psychotherapy and the anthropological study of marriage and courtship. Anthropologists' observations of the culture and of individuals, subgroups and families were confirmed by the evolution of family therapy and the study of the behavior, language and mythology of the family system. The field of family therapy has since expanded more and more with a series of theoretical frameworks and deeper understandings of the dynamics within the family.

As psychotherapy became both a healing art and a method for psychosocial research, the interfaces between the family system and its subsystems made the hierarchy of control more obvious. The authors of this book seem to have precipitated us into a new interface. They present the relationship between our social structure and the family. As the subsystems of our society become more urbanized, the pressure of neighbors and the community expectations, as enforced by the school system, the church system, and the political system, have precipitated a new set of power vectors. The individual's strength is largely derived from the early experience with his/her family. However, the power of the family, its stability, and its tolerance of change are massively responsive to the demands of the social structure. In Babylon anyone who became sick was forced to sit in the village square, and each citizen who walked by had to prescribe for the illness, and the patient had to carry out the prescription. In essence, that society was the doctor, and sickness was assumed to be within the control of the individual.

Adam and Eve inherited a good life. When they disobeyed the rules of their community, they became aware that they were naked. They were ashamed of not living up to the image of their creator. In our modern world the first commandment, "Thou shalt not worship a graven image," has been eroded by the culture, such that deliberately designing a favorable image has become an art and science of its own. It is as though we have resurrected the power of image worship and have made it a justifiable craft. We talk casually about plans for the president to change his image and be softer towards the Russians, to appear less conciliatory towards South Africa and act more concerned to his voting public.

To the farm boy growing up in isolation from the community, the dissonance between parental control and children's adventurous efforts was a personal struggle. The generation gap was taking place within the family. However, in the ghetto community of a modern city most parents add a collective reinforcement to the cross-generational struggle—"No son dares to act like that toward his mother." Thus, the mother introduces a third-person quality to the two-person struggle between the child and parent. In essence, she is saying, "You must adapt to our family ethos, but you must also be careful lest other people look down upon us and you, thereby, shame our whole family."

The need to dress correctly and to behave in an accepted way is thus separated from the personhood of the individual. If his family is healthy it does not reinforce the social demand for proper behavior but respects his personhood as the prime evidence of his worth. The reverse of shame is pride. The shameful experience is a sense of having failed to live up to one's projected image. If one dresses correctly, talks correctly, knows the right people, and lives up to the image other people respect, one is successful. One cartoonist showed the psychiatrist talking to an ex-patient and saying in indignation, "You still feel guilty after all these years of treatment? You ought to feel ashamed of yourself."

Guilt is the inner experience of breaking the moral code. Shame is the inner experience of being looked down upon by the social group. The essential difference is that shame, like pride, is related to the fantasy of oneself rather than to one's actual behavior. Pride is maintaining the fantasy, the delusion of grandeur, of the fantasy of being the envy of other people. Pride is not satisfaction with something accomplished but glorying in something dreamed of. Characteristically, both pride and shame are ways in which the individual is prevented from establishing his personhood. I suppose the ultimate victim of shame would be the king's son who by universal delusion was acknowledged to have no imperfections. Therefore, there was a whipping boy, a ghetto companion. Whenever the king's son did something that was not worthy of the image of perfection, the whipping boy was whipped to help the king's son face the shame of his violation of the nation's delusion of his perfection, as exemplified by the family and the people around him who live in the delusion of his image.

The authors seem to have discovered a new syndrome, which might be labeled "addiction to social conformity." The symptom of this addiction is any deviation from the community standard. In essence, the family has accepted these standards and the individual must conduct himself in such a way that he will be admired for upholding the community's image of itself and the family's image of itself. This triangulation is also rampant in our modern social structure. One is no longer given status in the community because of his personhood but stands or falls on the basis of his social creativity, social contribution or social usefulness. To say that President Carter was a person to be admired is secondary to the fact that he did not keep his image polished, and therefore, his presidency was less effective. In contrast, President Reagan is generally regarded as one who acts well, maintains an image of success, and therefore, is to be revered for it.

Shame is the result of a social crime, the disobeying of a social law, "Thou shall not only obey thy parent, thou shalt live up to the image that he has painted for the neighbors." The alcoholic, noted for his dishonesty, is one such social sinner. This could be described as his effort to provide a corrected, approved image. He believes he is in control of his alcohol problem and that his public image is correctable. All of his lies are little white lies. He is not sinful in the moral sense, and therefore, he is not guilty. He is merely disapproved of in the social sense. He is embarrassed and embarrassing.

Is this really a description of a new system syndrome? Whereas the family sets itself up as a prideful subgroup of the community and sets up its individual members as addicts to the pride of social conformity? The post-modern ethnographers are about to have a holiday integrating interfaces between the community, the family, the interpersonal world of twos and threes, and even the intrapsychic world of the individual. Furthermore, it is even possible that the exposure of this family community pattern may ask for more and more microscopic examination of the dynamics up and down the hierarchical system, just as this same phenomenon is taking place in the physical sciences and has made for massive research progress.

These authors then have worked a pattern of moving up the system's hierarchy to the community and its effect on the family and the family's individual members. This produces a peculiar kind of third-person degradation that they call shame. The public shadow induces a private horror. Is it possible that this peculiar symptom is the result of childhood experience with the family? Does this family live in a false pride relationship to the community and then utilize the individual member's family as scapegoats? If this is true, then by degrading the individual member of the family in the name of the community they protect their image. Are we about to discover a scheme that will clarify the social introject and its effect on the family? Are these authors leading us beyond the statistics of the sociologist and the fairly descriptive, photographic details of the anthropologist? If so, we may be at the entrance to a study of the collective unconscious of the community, as reflected in those hidden facets of some families who are destroyed by the reflections of the social sin and of the new religion of materialism and all of us — its social slaves.

Carl A. Whitaker, M.D.

INTRODUCTION

This book is about a dragon, a mythic monster called shame. Few people in our culture have escaped this creature, whose claws can lock us in a frozen state and devour our ability to verbalize.

The Chinese say that the dragon possesses the power of metamorphosis and the gift of rendering itself invisible. Shame's invisibility is powerful; yet, the invisible in life is what we long to know intimately. We believe in the metamorphosis of this dragon called shame. Just as a lump of coal gives off warmth and softness when ignited, so can a family transform its dynamics from shame to respect. Both have the potential for change; both need to be ignited. It is this metamorphosis which has held our constant attention. As families have had the courage to face the dragon, so have they changed their relationships. Bateson (1979) has stated that the pattern that connects is the pattern that corrects. This correcting pattern is the pattern for growth.

Reflecting on our early clinical recognition of shame as a family dynamic, we recall two vivid scenes. One scene focused on our initial awareness of shame and the other on our exploration of a definition.

In a therapy session, we observed a perplexing response to a now forgotten remark. A subtle "shadow" of coloring moved across the client's face, but her overall expression did not change and, in fact, seemed almost frozen. Her silent affective response signaled a much stronger feeling than embarrassment. We were confused: our small talk had not warranted such a powerful reaction. Sensing we had unintentionally tapped some hidden pain, one of us asked, "I have a hunch

x   Facing Shame

that what I just said triggered your experiencing shame; is
that accurate?" The client reddened, slowly nodded and responded, "Why, yes. I guess I didn't know there was a word
for this awful feeling. It happens quite often." A moment later
she gave a deep sigh of relief and we began talking about the
interaction and the source of her shame. As we agreed to explore this phenomenon in depth with her, we became aware
that something was happening not only in our client but also
in ourselves. We realized that we were not clear about why
we asked her about shame.

In reviewing the session together, we reflected on other clients upon whose faces we had seen that "shadow." This event
triggered our budding inquiry into shame.

As we turned our family lens to focus on shame, we found a
high correlation between shame and dependency in families
bound by and entangled in rigid, perfectionistic rule systems.
Many of the families entering therapy with us had been treated for chemical dependency or other addictions as well as
physical and sexual abuse. Shame seemed to be an organizing principle in these families' dynamics.

In discussing the concept of shame as a family issue, we
must place it in a context. We cannot know shame in a vacuum; the family is intricately woven into our country's social
fabric. We face at the family level that which prevails at the
societal or national level. Other institutions besides the family – the churches, schools and political systems – have participated in this dynamic of shame we see in families.

The result is that many people strive to live up to an impossible image of what others suggest or direct them to be.
The media – books, television and films – have long depicted
a romantic image of the family. When families fail to meet
the perfectionistic images, they feel inadequate and unworthy
and try harder with more control. When families' rule systems
incorporate those high degrees of control, the shame-bound
cycle is set in motion. Thus the societal standards affect the
psychodynamic domain of the family.

Shame is not limited to those easily recognized families
whose presenting stories include addiction. Shame is an experi-

ence common to many – people from all socioeconomic groups, from all ethnic backgrounds, and of all ages. No one is exempt from some shaming experiences in his or her lifetime. Further, shame is masked by a myriad of well-developed, sophisticated defense systems. A trusting therapeutic relationship is needed to remove these masks so that the underlying pain and shame become accessible to treatment.

As our awareness of shame increased, we began to see our own families with new insight. We realized that, quite naturally, we were facing personally what we were uncovering professionally. So we began our endeavors to unravel our family-of-origin myths and secrets and identify our own family pain and shame. Of course, in the process we came to view more clearly our own histories of shame and reached a deeper understanding of our past and present loyalty to family rules and myths. We had sought to keep our family images intact and, failing that, felt the pain of our own personhoods. What began as an exploration into our clients' shame became a very personal and equalizing process.

As we presented workshops on what we were learning about shame to other therapists, clergy, and educators, we frequently heard the comment, "I came to learn about my clients' shame, and I also learned about my own." It became clearer to us that we were recognizing a very pervasive phenomenon.

The second scene that stands out in our reflections on shame involves defining shame. During an afternoon chat with Carl Whitaker following a consultation, we asked for his thoughts on shame. Carl paused and then playfully responded, "Shame occurs when you haven't been able to get away with the 'who' you want people to think you are." Turning from his humorous response defining a "false self," he then went to the desk and read aloud the dictionary meaning of shame. The dictionary identified shame as a "painful mental condition." We then began our pursuit to deepen our definition of shame.

We turned to the literature to explore shame from three perspectives – philosophy, psychoanalysis, and ego psychology. We read about the "sense of shame," the cycle of shame-

guilt, and shame in ego identity. In focusing next on psychotherapy, we found the description of shame evolve from a
single cycle of shame-guilt (Piers & Singer, 1971) to an interpersonal examination (Kaufman, 1980) and also a description in the context of the family (Stierlin, 1974). We joined
theoretical company with some of our colleagues in distin-
guishing shame from guilt but over time made a distinct turn
in our approach to both.

Our definition of shame refers to humiliation so painful,
embarrassment so deep, and a sense of being so completely
diminished that one feels he or she will disappear into a pile
of ashes. Shame involves the entire self and self worth of a
human being.

While we agree with previous definitions of shame (Schneider, 1977), we take a positive approach toward its therapeutic value. We believe that when we face shame in a supportive environment, we are freed to strike out in new directions
on our journeys toward liberation and maturity. Our interpretation of guilt assumes the distinction between *neurotic
guilt*, which stems from family dynamics of anxiety and compulsivity, and *mature guilt*, which functions as the affective
barometer of conscience linked to our deepest values.

We have placed both shame and mature guilt on a continuum in a therapeutic model depicting the movement from
shame-bound family dynamics to respectful dynamics. In ap-
plying this model, we have found that facing shame reduces
dependence and helps shape identity, leading to a reduction
in addictive behaviors and obsessions. Personal freedom and
dignity are restored in this process.

In Chapter 1 we describe the clinical problem, define the
terms "shame" and "guilt," and discuss the implications of
shame for psychotherapists. We show that when shame is
understood in the context of the family system, the therapist
has a much more powerful model for family therapy.

In Chapter 2, we contrast the shame-bound family system
with the respectful family system. Each has characteristics
recognizable to therapists working with clients' shame issues.

The origins of shame and the ongoing patterns are described in Chapter 3. We define three stages of shame: external, inherited generational, and maintained. *External shame* is the event, often traumatic, that risks the family's public exposure and humiliation. The event can range from an embezzlement or job loss, resulting in loss of family pride, to an explicit sexual assault in the family. The family's secret protection of external shame results in *inherited generational shame*. *Maintained shame* presents itself as the clinical problem. It is the ongoing shame-bound dynamic that maintains the shame in the family and in its members' interpersonal patterns. We also include here the myriad ways in which shame is masked in families.

Chapter 4 explores the lack of boundary clarity at the family structural level, the marital/generational level, and the intrapsychic, or ego, level. Included in this chapter is an explanation of the "zipper" metaphor, which illustrates how personal boundaries are developed and maintained.

The implicit rules governing the recurrent interactional patterns in the shame-bound family are presented in Chapter 5. These eight rules can produce and maintain the shame-bound system.

We present our conceptual model of shame and control in Chapter 6. We illustrate the shame-bound cycle: control, release and shame.

Since addiction and shame are inseparable, in Chapter 7 we turn to the most frequently identified addictions we meet and work with. We include the dynamics of codependence and the role of therapeutic support systems, including 12-step programs.

In Chapter 8 we present the philosophical underpinnings of our therapeutic approach. We show the assumptions from which our therapeutic processes grow. Here we attempt to emphasize that our crises are opportunities for continued growth.

Chapter 9 describes the basic therapeutic interventions therapists can use in working with the shame-bound family. In this chapter we view the individual in the context of the family of origin concurrently with the person's present-day life problems, and describe the therapeutic process.

We acknowledge that our therapy model for family shame requires the therapist to use his or her personal relationship with clients. This approach often means long-term work, and while it does not fit well in brief therapy models, we have learned that the concepts can be encouraging and useful to any therapist in viewing another turn on the kaleidoscope of family therapy. When we break the family systems rule by talking openly about shame and break the invisible bond that has entrapped so many of us for so many years, we can take another step toward self-respect and integrity.

We frankly wonder if we have been able to convey what shame really is; it is our hope, however, that the stories told here can aid family therapists in meeting and understanding shame in families. Perhaps the quotation from author Mary Richards says it best: "We have to realize that a creative being lives within ourselves, whether we like it or not, and that we must get out of its way, for it will give us no peace until we do" (Richards, 1964, p. 27).

References

Bateson, G. (1979). *Mind and nature*. New York: Bantam Books.

Kaufman, G. (1980). *Shame*. Cambridge, MA: Schenkman Publishing.

Piers, G. & Singer, M. (1971). *Shame and guilt*. New York: Norton.

Richards, M. (1964). *Centering*. Middletown, CT: Wesleyan University Press.

Schneider, C. (1977). *Shame, exposure and privacy*. Boston: Beacon Press.

Stierlin, H. (1974). Shame and guilt in family relations. *Archives of General Psychiatry, 30*, 381–389.

ACKNOWLEDGMENTS

The completion of this book is a joyous occasion. It gives us the opportunity to pay special tribute to the many people who have taught us, supported us personally, and worked with us on the manuscript. Our professional family and co-therapists at the Family Therapy Institute, Rene Schwartz, Karen Johnson, Jim Jacobs, and David Keith, have participated in many important ways, listening to us, contributing ideas, and believing in what we were doing. Rene gave especially generously of her ideas and hours in reading the manuscript. David's helpful editorial suggestions are included throughout the book. Our support team would not be complete without Esther Davis, whose good-natured encouragement helps keep us organized. Jane Dickman is a fine person to have for a neighbor as well as an efficient secretary.

Our teachers have been many. We would like to name two who taught us so much and whose belief in us has helped us believe in ourselves, Virginia Satir and Carl Whitaker. They carry no responsibility for where we have gone with what we learned or what is presented in this book. We treasure their teaching and their friendship for the foundation it has provided us.

Mavis Fossum's patience and companionship over "book talk" have been as important as her reading and help with the manuscript. Special thanks to Duncan Stanton, Diane Dovenberg, Janet Tidemann, and Norma Rowe for their reading and suggestions.

We appreciate the expert assistance Kathleen Michels has given in honing our writing skills. Thanks to Kathryn Mickelson, the artist who breathed life into our illustrations.

We give special thanks to Susan Barrows, our editor, who has seen us through this work and believed in it from the beginning, and to Carl Whitaker who pointed us in her direction.

Facing Shame

FAMILIES IN RECOVERY

1

THE INVISIBLE DRAGON

When Cal and Judy* appeared for their first therapy appointment they were the embodiment of middle-class success. Cal, 31, was tall, with curly brown hair, and wore the pinstriped, vested, dark suit obligatory to his profession as a lawyer. His handshake was firm and assertive and his smile came easily. Judy, 30, was a tastefully dressed woman with strawberry blond hair and a pale complexion. Her two-piece suit, conservative makeup and hairstyle spoke of good taste and attention to detail. This would serve her well in the banking business where she was a promising young executive. Her manner in meeting us seemed somewhat more cool and reserved than Cal's, although she seemed eager to begin our session.

To open this first interview we asked what had led them to seek family therapy. They glanced at each other, raised their eyebrows, and Judy said, "Do you want to start or should I?" Cal gave her the nod to proceed. Now, as she settled into her chair, it was becoming clear to us that her model exterior was slightly betrayed by faint lines of fatigue around her eyes. She said their relationship had lost the loving feelings. As she talked, Cal gazed off into the distance, perhaps looking back in his mind to the times when their relationship

---

*Cal and Judy, like the other people mentioned in our case examples, are composites of many shame-bound individuals we have seen in our clinical practice. The experiences of shame-bound people are similar; any similarity of our examples to specific individuals is only a result of their typical characteristics.

felt more loving. But his aloofness lasted only until she began
to describe a specific disagreement that they had had three
nights before. Judy had stopped at the store on her way home
from work and picked up a bag of large prime grapefruit to
have for her breakfasts. Later that evening, she walked into
the kitchen and found Cal sitting at the table eating one of
them.

Cal broke in sharply on Judy's description at this point,
saying, "Wait a minute. How many times have you eaten
something that I brought home for myself? I don't ever make
a big deal out of it because I think we ought to share what
we have."

Now it was Judy's turn to be offended. She pleaded that
he was not getting her point at all. She had bought those
grapefruit for her own use and he had "stolen" one for his own
selfish purposes without asking!

Their argument had fierce emotional intensity and a stir-
ring fervor, but it lacked any movement toward resolution.
They continued to throw verbal charges at each other, sometimes glaring with intense hate; then they'd catch each other's
eye and there would be a hint of a silly, flirtatious grin. This
was intensity without meaning and without depth. It was the
sort of fight which seemed to exist for its own sake and for
the intense sense of abandon in the contact (painful as it was),
rather than for resolution of differences. We quickly saw that
we were going to have to work hard as therapists to even get
noticed in their all-consuming interchange. These people had
learned how to be successful in their career roles and public
relationships, but in the intimacy of personal relationships
they were like undeveloped beginners, that is, like children.

It was significant to us that as they escalated the intensity of their interaction, they failed to move closer to an exchange of meaning or to a resolution. He called her a "selfish
bitch" and she called him a "phony wimp." As therapists we
had seen enough at this point, or more than enough to know
the viciousness in their relationship. We raised our voices
now to interrupt this hopeless interaction, and when we had
their attention asked, "How long have you been using these
assaultive methods on each other?"

Each put up a mild defense and then seemingly collapsed like a shameful child. Cal hung his head and averted his eyes. Judy became tearful and talked about herself as a hopeless person. "I would like to drop through a trapdoor right now and disappear."

What we see on the surface in the example of Judy and Cal is a couple who get into the most petty and childish fights. It is sadly painful for them to live this way. Yet, the intensity of their fighting (more than the fighting itself) holds some sort of grip on them – a payoff for their pain. They are living under the constraints imposed by a shame-bound family rule system. Their set of rules for interaction prevents the development of any sense of real personhood. Instead they develop a sense of shame, of being depersonalized and bad or hollow.

We define shame in experiential terms. It is more than loss of face or embarrassment. *Shame is an inner sense of being completely diminished or insufficient as a person. It is the self judging the self. A moment of shame may be humiliation so painful or an indignity so profound that one feels one has been robbed of her or his dignity or exposed as basically inadequate, bad, or worthy of rejection. A pervasive sense of shame is the ongoing premise that one is fundamentally bad, inadequate, defective, unworthy, or not fully valid as a human being.*

We distinguish between the terms "guilt" and "shame." Guilt is the developmentally more mature, though painful, feeling of regret one has about behavior that has violated a personal value. Guilt does not reflect directly upon one's identity nor diminish one's sense of personal worth. It emanates from an integrated conscience and set of values. It is the reflection of a developing self. A person with guilt might say, "I feel awful seeing that I did something which violated my values." Or the guilty person might say, "I feel sorry about the consequences of my behavior." In so doing the person's values are reaffirmed. The possibility of repair exists and learning and growth are promoted. While guilt is a painful feeling of regret and responsibility for one's actions, shame is a painful feeling about oneself as a person. The possibility for

repair seems foreclosed to the shameful person because shame
is a matter of identity, not a behavioral infraction. There is
nothing to be learned from it and no growth is opened by the
experience because it only confirms one's negative feelings
about oneself.

For many people shame exists passively without a name.
Its origins are in identity development or in the premises of
"who I am." The roots of shame are in abuse, personal violations, seductions and assaults where one's sense of self has
been trampled, one's boundaries defiled. What remains may
be only an ache. There are no words for the absence of an af-
firmation of self, as shame often is. How do we say, "I fail to
affirm my worthiness to myself"? The more active experience
of shame does have words, like, "stupid," "weakling," "weird,"
"sickie."

Upon meeting Judy and Cal we saw several characteristics
in a pattern suggesting that we were dealing with a shame-
bound family system. Their individual feelings of shame were
not prominent in their *awareness* because they had fulfilled
the dominant culture's recipe for success. This shell of apparent success covered an underlying sense of being undeveloped and diminished as persons. The family pattern in this
kind of system may be discouraging and often overwhelming for therapists as well as family members. Yet, when we
recognize the familiar qualities in the pattern of the shame-
bound system, we have hope for our work with people. Seeing the pattern has pointed the way to formulation of effective and meaningful therapeutic approaches.

Some of the recognizable characteristics of the shame-
bound system exemplified by Cal and Judy are: 1) *the mix-
ture of control and chaos* seen in the contrast between their
public effectiveness and their privately chaotic lives; 2) *the
personally blaming and disqualifying messages* seen in the
name-calling and in the repeated failure to hear the meaning
of each other's communication, intermixed with disqualifying flirtatiousness; 3) *the verbal and nonverbal statements of
shame* as seen in averted eyes, lowered head, slumped shoulders, and feeling like a "hopeless person"; 4) *the failure to com-*

plete transactions seen in their lack of resolution and seemingly endless resentment; 5) *the therapists' subjective sense of mystification or missing pieces* in the interview – we had the strong subjective sense that what was being talked about as "the problem" simply did not "add up."

THE PRESENTING PROBLEMS

When clients appear at the psychotherapist's office they commonly have some clarity about the immediate event or pressure or personal pain which has precipitated this visit. They may be motivated by a personal sense of failure in marriage, a legal directive from a judge in court, a referral from their physician, or a worrisome behavior of their child. However, they will not come with a list of all the symptoms or all the behaviors which a therapist will consider to be central to their problems. All people have behaviors, assumptions, and lifestyles which they simply take for granted and which provide the unconscious stage for their daily life.

Family rules, personal behaviors which support the rules, and individual loyalty to the system fall largely into this unconscious category. For example, a family rule might be, "Don't make your needs obvious." Behaviors supporting the rule might be much bravado in the family interaction, stealing, and suppressed loneliness. Their loyalty might be expressed as "this is the way most families are," or "this is the only way I can do it." These stage-setting variables form the underlying ground upon which individual family members stand and join them to one another in a family group. While each family system has its own unique pattern forming its stage, as family therapists we look for *patterns of patterns* which allow us to generalize about families.

That is what we have done in uncovering patterns of shame. Early in our learning we thought we were dealing with distinctly different problems – one family having a problem with alcohol abuse, another with compulsivity around money, and another with physical abuse. The separate family patterns came together in a pattern, a template of shame. We learned that issues of shame form a theme which exists as a stage beneath many of the problems brought to a therapist's doorstep. Usually the particular pain or pressure identified by the client is a side effect or a product of the system. It is the family therapist's task to explore the stage on which they stand. The concept of the shame-bound family system provides a much more powerful therapeutic model than we previously had for uncovering and treating a wide array of these problems.

As we define the term, *a shame-bound family is a family with a self-sustaining, multigenerational system of interaction with a cast of characters who are (or were in their lifetime) loyal to a set of rules and injunctions demanding control, perfectionism, blame and denial. The pattern inhibits or defeats the development of authentic intimate relationships, promotes secrets and vague personal boundaries, unconsciously instills shame in the family members, as well as chaos in their lives, and binds them to perpetuate the shame in themselves and their kin.* It does so regardless of the good intentions, wishes, and love which may also be part of the system.

Judy and Cal, the couple presented at the beginning of this chapter, displayed in their interaction the patterns of the shame-bound system. The pain they could express, which motivated them to seek therapy, was in their marital relationship. We knew from the pattern we saw that our effectiveness and efficiency in helping them have a more loving, intimate relationship would be greatly enhanced by exploring the origins of their shame-bound system.

Our initial learning about the family system bound in shame came through our studies of families with an addicted member. A strong community focus on alcoholism led us to look at these families with new awareness. At that time we used the term "alcoholic family." Many of the characteristics which we now identify broadly as hallmarks of the shame-bound family we first thought were specific to families with alcohol and drug addiction. In retrospect it is clear that we were becoming acquainted with a much broader and more pervasive syndrome than anything limited to chemical addiction. Combining the perspective brought from family therapy with a concern about alcoholism proved to be a very generative mix. The study of families with an alcohol problem provided a passkey to the broader issue of shame in families.

Once the pattern of this system became recognizable to us, we would see the pattern in a family and then ask ourselves, "Where's the addiction?" Often, the question led us to a chemical addiction in the family which had not been identified. Sometimes the addiction was not manifest in the current nuclear family at all, but had been a prominent feature in the childhood family of one or both of the adults. So that led us to the next awareness, that the characteristic system could be continued into subsequent generations independently of any active addiction. Many of the adult children of alcoholics have been helped by this learning. They could grow from the therapeutic approach used with "alcoholic families," even though there was no alcoholism in the current generation, because the shame-bound family system is multigenerational and self-sustaining.

In other families we would ask ourselves, "Where's the addiction?" and although the characteristic pattern was clearly present, there was no evidence of chemical addiction in this generation or previous ones. What the "passkey" opened to us was a systemic pattern which is a stage for many forms of human pain and misery, not limited to chemical addiction. We find themes of the shame-bound family when people are *compulsively abusing themselves* in all the countless ways they can do so: abusing drugs and alcohol, physically inflicting pain or injury, overworking, overexercising, or starving themselves. We recognize the same theme when people are *compulsively abusing others*, whether it be child abuse or spouse abuse and whether the abuse be physical, sexual, or emotional.

The pattern is recognizable in many different behaviors which we have come to identify as compulsive. They include *compulsions related to money and material goods*, such as compulsive shopping, overspending, hoarding, saving, and shoplifting. They include many *compulsions related to sexuality*, such as compulsive voyeurism, exhibitionism, masturbation, affairs and casual encounters, use of pornography, obscene phone calls, incest and rape. This host of compulsive behaviors includes *compulsions related to food*, as in anorexia nervosa, bulimia, obsessive dieting and overeating. We are also coming to see the shame-bound system as a recognizable pattern in *agoraphobia* and some *psychosomatic* problems.

Often the compulsive nature of these behaviors has not been recognized by either the client or the therapist. In other instances therapists have refused to consider the behavior compulsive on the principle that they were determined to hold the client responsible for his or her own behavior. We, of course, hold people responsible for their behavior. When compulsivity is identified, it provides a direction for treatment which allows a person to *effectively* take on responsibility. It provides a way to face the shame directly and change the elements of the system which maintain the shame.

We have come to see a host of compulsive behaviors in a new way: as addictions in a systemic sense, even though there is no physical, organic dependency. These compulsions or addictions are found to cluster in the families of the shame-bound system and in some instances seem to be almost interchangeable with one another. As one of the behaviors is controlled or moves into the background, another may replace it. They are conditions which arise within the system and by their compelling nature act as central pillars to maintain the status quo within the system. In any given family with a strongly developed shame process, one may see a whole cluster of these symptoms in the individual members, some more pronounced and others more subtle.

As an example, an identified patient seeking help might present sadness and depression as the point of pain motivating the request for therapy. But, to understand the dynamic of her pain we explore her family system and find that she had an alcoholic and abusive father; there are other current symptoms in the family which have gone unidentified, such as a husband who is compulsively overeating and overspending and a child who is shoplifting. All of these symptoms interlock, arising in turn upon the stage of the shame-bound family and serving to maintain the system. A therapist attempting to treat her depression while disregarding the family system is working with too small a piece of the truth. A family therapist might be asked to enter the family through any one of these windows of family pain while the other symptoms remain unnoticed or unmentioned.

THE PROBLEM MAINTAINS THE SYSTEM

When the therapeutic goal is to change the system of a shame-bound family, it is vitally important to identify compulsive, abusive, or phobic behaviors if they are present. Until these behaviors are identified and dealt with directly, the dehumanizing and shaming aspects of the system will be sustained. It has repeatedly been our experience in a therapeutic process that a client may be making very slow progress or none at all. Then, in the evolution of the therapy, it is revealed that a particular shame-based behavior has been kept secret or hasn't been acknowledged as significant. That moment in therapy is a breakthrough because the behavior, although not the original cause for shame, serves a vital role in maintaining the equilibrium of the system and the shame of the people involved.

In our original case example, Judy and Cal were open and direct about the constant fighting and power struggles in their relationship. The mistrust and hurt feelings were rampant. What they never addressed directly with each other, much less with their therapists, was the fact that they had much secrecy and mystification in their relationship. Cal's relationship to money and spending was the first of the compulsions to unravel in therapy. His pattern was to buy things he didn't need and couldn't use or afford. He would build up big charge accounts and try to keep them secret from Judy. Judy would try to trust Cal because she was ashamed to be a suspicious wife. Yet she was secretly checking up on his purchases, keeping track of what new tools and new clothes he had and indirectly asking about them. Periodically this would all come to a head and they would have a big fight about money, but there was never any resolution of substance. The fighting would stop by distraction or exhaustion and they would both resume their secret, indirect behavior. Neither Judy nor Cal knew that this was a compulsion.

The therapists, unaware of the buying pattern, were working with them on their communication issues, self-esteem and autonomy, all of which were pertinent to their problems. No significant movement or new learning took place over the weeks of therapy until the reality of compulsive spending was opened up. It happened after they had another explosion in their relationship. In the session Judy apologized to Cal for even bringing it up because she knew it would upset him. She told us that a collection agency had appeared at the door with a loan in Cal's name amounting to over $20,000. She had never been told of the loan before. Cal was very shameful about and furious at Judy for exposing his "business issues" in therapy. He claimed to not know where all the money had been spent. In piecing together this story we insisted that Cal begin to account, in detail, for where he had spent the money. He actually didn't know himself where much of it was spent because his compulsive, addictive pattern was to hide the reality from himself by ignoring it. Clearly, he was not in control of his spending behavior. No substantial progress would take place until he acknowledged this problem and his need to work on it. Equally important was Judy's compulsive focus on Cal and Cal's problem, foreclosing her own development of her own responsible subjectivity.

When the therapy process gets stuck or bogged down in a circular repetitive form, it is a clue that there may be some shame-based, compulsive behavior which hasn't been adequately addressed. In some instances there is a sense of progress but it is nebulous and never comes to conclusion until the obsessive, compulsive, abusive, or phobic behavior gets confronted. Traditional psychodynamics direct us to look for the motivation, the dynamic need or historical basis for the behavior. That theoretical position says that when neurotic need is resolved in therapy it no longer exists as a need. The behavior ceases when it has no function. We find this position to be inadequate to understanding shame-bound systems.

What we are observing is a runaway system which continues its behavior, intensifies it, and ritualizes it, totally detached from the original motivation. The individuals continue the behavior and are not free to stop by their own rational decision. A central question which has concerned family therapists, especially those of the Palo Alto group, is: "Why do families stay the same?" This creative question takes us beyond the search for an original cause of a problem. It implies an ongoing process in the present which maintains a pattern. In looking at the shame-bound system we see that kind of self-sustaining process.

The coping responses within the system serve only to intensify the problem. Then the intensified problem serves to intensify the coping responses. The shame-bound system, once in motion, tends to stay in motion under its own momentum. The original motivation or need for the behavior is no longer an active dynamic. Relevance of historical origins and work with them is not discarded in the therapeutic process once the train has been stopped. Usually these origins are in victimization and misfortune in the past. First to be addressed in therapy, however, is the runaway system in the present.

The shame-bound cycle shown in Figure 1 is a way of conceptualizing this self-sustaining process. It will be discussed more fully in Chapter 6. At this point we will introduce the hypothetical cycle to explain what we mean by "the problem maintains the system."

First we are going to examine how *individuals* within the family move on the cycle. Later we will discuss the implications for the system as a whole. Each position on the cycle supports and intensifies the other position. The control phase makes the release phase more likely and more intense. The intensified release phase calls for more control. Shame is pictured at the hub of this destructive process, driving it, organizing it, and intensifying both phases. The release phase, either by its chaotic nature or its violation of the control values, adds to the shame. The control phase feels like a refuge from shame, but is actually only a hiding place and covers the shame. Shame increases from the loss of control or loss of personal dignity or integrity in the release phase

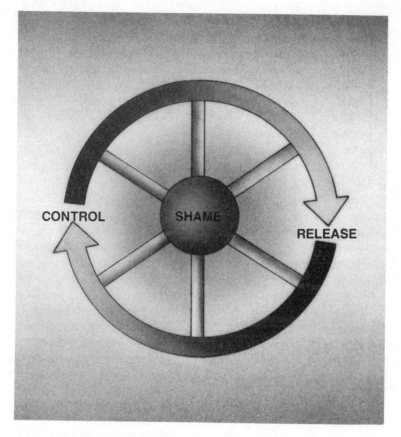

Figure 1 Shame-bound cycle

and intensifies the control and reform which follows. Each phase on the cycle is a coping response to the other. Control and release may be natural human rhythms, but when organized and intensified by shame they become intense, out of control, and destructive polarities.

Some simplified examples of individuals will illustrate the process. A father in the control phase is careful, tense about his parenting, and trying hard to do it right. He may be very demanding of his children or critical of them and is looking to them for validation that he's doing a good job. In the release phase he breaks out in anger and frustration, verbally or physically abusing them. His shame about himself as a father is enhanced by this abusive behavior and he is appalled at what he has done. He may try to cover it up or minimize it, blame it on someone else, or resolve that it will never happen again. His shame leads to more resolutions to do better in the future, which are manifest in a return to an intensified control phase.

In another example a woman is anxious about her physical health. She obsesses about it and thinks about controlling her activities day and night so as not to threaten or jeopardize her well-being. Her basic shame and this intense focus on her physical health seem inevitably to lead to self-doubts and anxiety about the most normal of physical sensations. As her tension builds, she perhaps confuses her need to feel all right as a person with a need for reassurance that she is all right physically. She goes to a physician for the reassurance. At the moment she hears that the doctor has found nothing physically wrong or that whatever was found will be treated, she is greatly relieved. This constitutes the release phase. It is followed by a sense of shame that she lost confidence in herself and went another time to the doctor when nothing was physically wrong. She hides or minimizes actions, decides she will try harder not to do it again and is now in the control phase.

The cycle tends to get stereotyped and ritualized. One person develops a reliable relationship with a chemical for the release while another person has a ritualized sexual behavior and another an eating behavior or a spending behavior.

In looking at the shame-bound system as a whole, we see all people in the system getting swept into this powerful process. The abusive behavior of one family member is the victimization and shame induction of another. In the release phase the addict loses himself or herself in the "high" of the mood swing. Simultaneously, other family members lose themselves in worry about the troublesome behavior of the addict. People within the system seem to borrow from one another's position on the cycle, i.e., one member of the family is often specialized in the control functions (doing everything right, keeping things together) while another member is specialized in the release functions (getting into difficulty, being "irresponsible"), and they balance each other. While everyone in the system has internalized shame, one of them often is the expresser or the embodiment of it by acting out in delinquency, poor achievement, or other so-called bad behavior, freeing the rest to express its polar opposite, propriety and goodness. Kaufman (1980, p. 23) gives an example of a mother repeatedly accusing her daughter of embarrassing her, thereby fostering a "pernicious tie . . . between the two of them which taught [the daughter] to experience herself merely as an extension of her mother, never as a separate person in her own right responsible for her own behavior."

Uncovering the shame and any particular behaviors representing ritualized patterns of control and release are prerequisite to disrupting the self-sustaining, dehumanizing pattern. This is often crucial whether or not the behaviors are a problem in and of themselves. Compulsive handwashing or compulsive masturbation is not a problem except as it affects the rest of one's life. Identifying specific release phase or control phase ritualized behaviors is not of much value in itself, but serves as an entry point for disrupting the central pillars of a dehumanizing or shaming system. After the behavior has been identified and interrupted, the cycle is disabled (or partially disabled) and each individual is more available to look at his or her own autonomy within the system.

As therapy progressed with Judy and Cal, Cal admitted that his buying and spending behavior was beyond his ability to control by force of will or rational decision. He described many occasions when he had gone into a shop "just to look around" and came out with numerous items which he didn't need and never did use. If an item were on sale, he sometimes bought two or three. Much of his unused material was hidden in secret hiding places in his garage and in the basement. He accepted some temporary external controls on his use of money as part of therapy. He asked a friend to participate with him in all check-writing transactions, decisions about how much pocket money to withhold from his salary check and any larger financial activity. Thus, he did not move into the control phase alone nor did he borrow Judy's control for himself, but temporarily turned the control decisions over to his friend. Further, his acknowledgment of not being in control meant that at least for several months he would not even enter a store alone.

The admission of his problem and acceptance of concrete practical help with it dramatically changed Cal's participation in the therapy sessions. Since his denial had crumbled he felt frightened and empty without his former habit to distract him. At the same time he eagerly engaged in working on his own responsibility for himself and his role in the relationship with Judy. He was referred to the self-help group for spenders called "Spenders Anonymous," which is based upon the 12-step program of Alcoholics Anonymous. It is a fellowship of people struggling with similar compulsions who follow a recovery program first developed by and for alcoholics in the late 1930s.

Judy too was shaken by the revelation of what she had only vaguely known before. At first she was angry about all the deceit. She had often felt there must be something wrong with her for feeling as she did. At the same time she was faced with her complicity in Cal's self-destructive behavior. Often she had observed that it put him in a good mood when he went shopping and she would point out sales he might like to check on. On the one hand she had shamed him for his loose manner with money and his secretiveness about it. On the other hand she had encouraged him to go shopping, to look for something for himself or the household, because she saw that it changed his mood positively.

Concurrently it came out that Judy had a history of a very compulsive relationship to food. Although it was much more under control now, in past years she was seriously underweight from dieting. At that time her physician was concerned enough about the health effects to consider hospitalization for her. Judy grew up in a household with a father who got drunk every weekend, and her whole family had been organized around trying to keep father on a even keel. So she had many shame and control issues to work on. As this information surfaced she felt shaken and more inclined to be in therapy for her own growth and less for Cal's improvement.

This compulsive process had profoundly affected the marriage in ways that neither of them had ever identified. Over the years, when real issues came up for them to deal with, each found a way to go around them by using the spending or dieting. In that way there was no deepening of their rapport, no building of mutual understanding from one issue or conflict to the next. While each felt unconsciously threatened by his or her own lack of control in specific areas, both gravitated to controlling responses as the single answer. Not only did their relationship fail to grow and deepen, but also they as individuals failed to mature in the process of interacting with normal life challenges and experiences. Being and becoming a person is a difficult, insecure process. We must continue to face that throughout our lives. We learn how to become a person through the process of intimate relationships with our families and friends. When a chronic means of avoiding and controlling those stresses has been found, it seriously limits our emotional and maturational development.

If human dignity and justice are universal human problems, then there are themes of shame at some level in all human systems. For many troubled families it is the central roadblock to growth and fulfillment; for others it is only a peripheral issue in the problems they have. Confrontation and exposure of compulsive, addictive, abusive or phobic behavior may be a very upsetting experience, even in discovering that it was manifested a generation or two ago or uncovering one's victimization decades in the past. In and of itself this is not enough. Facing the hidden dragon, shame, which may rise to the surface in the confrontation, is the beginning of a productive therapy experience. The dragon becomes the stepping-stone. It brings within reach real therapeutic growth and true changes in a family system.

Reference

Kaufman, G. (1980). *Shame: The power of caring*. Cambridge, MA: Shenkman Publishing Co.

2

CONTRASTING RESPECTFUL
AND SHAME-BOUND SYSTEMS

A shame-bound family is a group of people, all of whom feel alone together. To the individuals in the family, shame feels unique and lonely; however, a systems perspective reveals that probably everyone feels his or her own version of uniqueness and loneliness. The shame which feels so peculiar to the self paradoxically is a product not of the individual and his or her unworthiness but of the system. The family system in which relationships are bound up in shame tends to demand that experience and people be judged on a goodness-badness scale. Within the family secrecy is rampant and relationships are thin and brittle.

The shame-bound family system is fixed in its form and highly resistant to change, even though change is a natural fact of life. This system is analogous to peanut brittle, with each person fixed in stereotyped, inflexible roles and relationships to one another. Change comes to all families in endless form and variation – as the birth of a child, or a child's growing into a more independent level of maturity, someone's getting ill, job and school changes, emancipation, separation and loss, death. When change exerts enough force all at one moment upon a rigid system, it may break and splinter. The shame-bound system does not have good capacity to absorb very much stress and still retain its integrity. These families may come to therapy before any yielding to change has occurred, or at the moment of stress when accommodation to change is simultaneously being demanded and resisted, or years after the splintering and all awareness of relevant relationship has been lost.

A respectful system has more variety and resilience in interpreting life experience because the flow of life events will be perceived more on their own merits than as a judgment of the person. Relationships have substance and resilience in the respectful system. People talk openly with one another about their lives rather than manage their relationships with secrets. They are openly vulnerable and dependent or needy at times without judgment. In the flow of their lives they learn deeply about each other as persons because pain is not denied or judged. Thus they are equipped to accommodate to the changes which inevitably and continuously come.

The respectful system is like tough leather. It has resilience. The losses are no less painful, the changes no less forceful. But it has greater capacity to absorb more of the stresses of change and still retain its integrity.

James is a school child who is part of a shame-bound family. On his way home from school one day he is taunted and struck by a "bully" classmate. This injustice is a shaming experience that can happen to any child from any family system. James' system has taught him to judge himself and his experience on a good-bad scale. He feels robbed of his dignity and feels that he is bad. When he arrives home he tells no one about what happened to him. His response is dysfunctional for his growth, not because he feels the pain of having been treated abusively, but because he keeps the incident and his feelings secret. To reveal it would be to reveal his vulnerability and open him to further judgment. In the secrecy his shame deepens because he is alienated from the support of his family.

In contrast, David, whose family system is more respectful and open and tends to enhance self-esteem, has the same experience on his way home from school. He bursts into his house yelling, "A terrible thing just happened to me!" He reacts with indignation to the assault, and as he does, he simultaneously feels the benefit of the supportive relationships and extends and deepens them. In effect, he expels the shame he feels and matures in his relationships.

DIMENSIONS OF RESPECT AND SHAME

Family systems fall somewhere along a continuum ranging from respectful to shame-bound. A system with patterns of interaction based upon accepting people as they are – not as they "should" be – open communication, and accountability will fall on the respectful end of the continuum and, in general, will have more fulfilled and emotionally well members. The most disturbed families tend to be the most extreme in their shaming and most victimized by it. Probably no family is at either absolute pole on this continuum. All families have a mix. (For a comparison of respectful and shame-bound systems, see Table 1.)

We distinguish between respectful and shame-bound systems in three ways.

TABLE 1
Contrasting Respectful and Shame-Bound Systems

Respectful Systems	Shame-Bound Systems
Violation of values leads to guilt.	Violation of person leads to shame.
Self is separate and part of a larger system.	Self has vague personal boundaries.
Rules require accountability.	Rules require perfectionism.
Relationship is dialogue.	Relationship is always in jeopardy.
Produce individuals with: accountability, repair, resolution;	more shame, despair;
deepening and modification of values, overtime;	increasing rigidity;
growing empathy;	alienation and distance;
growth of self as a whole person.	development of an image and of control.

1) Violation of values versus violation of person

The origin of respectful guilt is an awareness of having violated one's values, standards, or rules. This painful feeling affirms that, "I am a person who holds this value. I violated my word or my agreement or my value and I need to make a correction, make repair, take responsibility, or be forgiven."

The origin of shame is in the violation and diminution of personhood. We worked with a very shameful client in therapy and as he was progressing we reflected to him how difficult it had been for him to feel like a good person when he first began therapy. His poignant reply was, "Good person, hell! I didn't feel like a person! I don't know what I felt like, if I felt like some animal or what – but I sure didn't feel like I was a human being!" This expresses the experience of many people who are chronically overwhelmed with shame. It is more profound than feeling lonely or cut off from others.

From the shame perspective, a person feels qualitatively different from other human beings, not really a full-fledged member of the human race. The story in the Bad Seed (March, 1967) is a good metaphor of shame because in some way that little girl was inherently unlike other children and not amenable to the socialization process. No matter what anyone did, her fundamental badness was bound to come forth. An experience of shame which is less overwhelming may be expressed as "second-class citizen," that is, one who does not have all of the rights to make mistakes and claim the privileges that everyone else has.

2) Self as separate and part of a larger system versus self with vague boundaries

The family system on the respectful end of the continuum shares among its members a perspective on self as being related and part of the universe. Children are acculturated into this perspective as they develop within the network of relationships. It implies a place where one can belong – not the central place but a place within a network of give-and-take relationships. It has been said that humility is knowing one's place and taking it. In that sense this system helps its members to have a self-respecting humility. The members of these families participate in the world around them. They have personal relationships within their neighborhood, workplace, school, synagogue, or church.

Parents in this system provide clear limits for their children's behavior as well as clear permission for other behavior. In this system the child learns reciprocity in the world. The child is seen as neither hero nor property but as a fellow human being on his or her own journey through life.

The family system on the shame end of the continuum shares among its members vague or distorted personal boundary definitions that inhibit development of a mature self. Members of this system tend to be very self-focused. Personal maturity and depth are undeveloped. In place of the system nourishing a mature sense of a strong self, shame undermines such development and a compensatory regime of extremes and denial seems to evolve. We find either rigid, shallow boundaries or mushy, undefined boundaries.

In the shame system with rigidly defined boundaries, the development of self gets cut off early. Children learn to value defiant individualism over the ongoing dialogue of relationship. Some families in this group are "liberal" and hold values of openness, but in practice we would call them pseudo-open because as they practice non-interference with one another, they ignore human dependency needs and resist genuine closeness in relationships. High priority is placed on being independent of thought and action, on not needing anyone, on being nonjudgmental to the extreme of "anything goes." The children especially are left wanting in their development of a self. They are given messages to think for themselves before they have learned from the modeling of others. These children are not given the opportunity to integrate the models which come from intimate knowing of others in their lives. These are the children who look back and say, "I think my father cared about me but I really never knew what he was like." We have seen the children of these families in our offices expressing anger and defiance or selfish, outrageous demands while their puzzled parents try harder to support their individuality. In the faces of these children one often sees the look of lost, unguided waifs.

Virginia Satir's (1972) concept of the self-other dilemma is helpful in understanding this family. This dilemma refers to the human conflict between needs of self-interest and the need to be in relationship with others. People who overvalue individualism never learn to resolve that dilemma. They never develop a resilient and deep sense of self because the value of individualism takes a singular position in their lives and the inherent tension with natural human dependency is avoided by denying it. When a family system can allow both individualism and dependency, the dialogue of this self-other dilemma within relationship produces a resolution which we call personal growth.

Another way in which the shame-bound family may develop distorted boundary definitions has been called by Bowen (1978) the undifferentiated family ego mass. Here separateness of the individual is denied and dependency has unchallenged validity. People assume a right or a need to interfere with each other's individual lives. One man who was visiting his mother in a distant city found her to be intruding on his plans for which friends he would see and what he would be doing for entertainment during his visit. She was saying things like, "You don't want to see those people but I think it's essential that you see these old friends. That museum isn't worth your brief time here so forget about that!" He protested that he would make his own plans and she should "bug off." She replied, "Don't try to be so independent!" This demonstrated for him the boundary invasiveness he had experienced in his family of origin.

The topic of boundaries is discussed more fully in Chapter 4.

3) Accountability versus perfectionism

The family that promotes self-respect shares a system of accountability among its members which provides for commitment, fulfillment of obligation, repair of wrongs, and for-

giveness. If a wife tells her husband she will meet him for dinner at 5:30, forgets and doesn't show up until 6:30, there is no dispute in this family that she did indeed let him down. He probably feels angry about it, and she probably feels the pain of guilt, having said one thing and failed to fulfill her commitment. But this system assumes that people are imperfect. It is understood that the husband had a right to expect his wife to appear when she said she would and that she is now obligated to make repair in order to restore the balance of give and take in their relationship. In this instance the repair may be accomplished simply by an apology and a more prompt appearance for future appointments.

The important distinction here is that, while the system expects direct acknowledgment of wrongs committed and repairs made, it doesn't attack the person's worth. When a parent assigns a task to a child and the child avoids it, the parent in this system holds the child accountable to complete it. The balance of give and take in the relationship is unresolved until the task is done by the child. It is respectful of the parent to give age-appropriate responsibility to the child and then hold the child accountable to complete it. The repair provides for self-respect, whereas the failure to repair in the event that the parent does the task instills shame. More simply stated, it is shaming when parents drop a reasonable expectation that was given to a child.

The shame-bound family is perfectionistic. The absoluteness of perfectionism does not provide for repair. There are only two categories for people: perfect and imperfect. One is either in the perfect category or one is outside of that category and less than acceptable. The important point to notice here is that within this system there is no way back, no repair available or relevant. A strike against you is a strike against you forever. Within this system mistakes can be brought up to a person years after they were committed. There is little or no resolution of wrongs or restoration of balance in relationships. Failures and hurts are inevitable in any close relationship but they seem to just dangle. They accumulate along with the accompanying power struggles, anger, and resentment.

Within this system of perfectionism, there may be great stress placed on control and doing things right. People are very anxious within the system, as they live under the control and demand to be right and do right. The motto within the system may be "Anything worth doing is worth doing right," or "If I want something done right I have to do it myself," or "I can't do it well enough so I won't try." Anything can be viewed through the lens of moral judgment. Eating, cleaning, school grades, personal grooming, having money and how it is used, even physical health and mental health are subject to moral monitoring on this perfectionistic standard.

While a system is functioning on a perfectionistic standard, those expectations may or may not be spelled out explicitly. It is common to see families in which this "perfect" standard exists as a vague "should." In those families, even the standard, as rigid as it is, cannot be used as a map or recipe for success within the family value system because it is too difficult to decipher. The children are not told clearly what is expected of them but they are a constant disappointment. In contrast, some families do spell out what is expected and the rules may be rigid, but the clarity provides a readable roadmap for how a child can be successful in that family. A common pitfall in the perfectionistic family is that expectations are clearly spelled out but they are so numerous that they are conflicting or paradoxical, or so unrealistic and controlling that they do not serve as a useful guide for behavior but only as a means of condemning.

Commonly there is conflict between the parents about standards and expectations for the children's behavior. The conflict may be explicit or very covert but it tends to go unresolved and paralyzes the parents in their parenting function. Minuchin and his colleagues described this dynamic in *Psychosomatic Families* (1978).

One family came to our office because the parents were concerned about their 18-year-old son's alcohol use and his recurrent failure in most of his high school classes, despite above-average intelligence. Rigid perfectionism, shame, anger, and failure to resolve differences were hallmarks of the parents' lives. The mother was a meticulous and thorough full-time homemaker, and the father in his profession as computer designer was devoted to detail. Mother was constantly "disappointed" in her son's lack of concern for keeping his room clean, his failure to hang up the clothes she had so carefully pressed for him, and his generally slovenly behavior. But she only gave him weak complaints and protests. She never affirmatively spelled out expectations, in part because her husband thought she was far too meticulous about the housekeeping and he took his son's side.

The father never really spelled out any expectations for the son at all. He had made an about-face in his rule-giving six years earlier when another son was killed by a car as he crossed the street. The father had directed the son to be home by 2:30 and the accident happened at 2:25 while he was coming home to comply with father's deadline. The accident report indicated that the son had used bad judgment in crossing the street in front of an oncoming car. The father concluded his son was rushing to meet the deadline, which had been rigidly set. This was clearly a demoralized family. The parents were immobilized in their parenting functions, yet they maintained their perfectionistic standards for themselves in their lives. In effect, the son was deprived of clear guidelines that would show him how to be successful in his parents' eyes. The only option available to him seemed to be failure.

The chaotic version of this system does not hold up standards or spell out expectations of any kind. There is little development of self among the family members because no structure exists to give direction for growth. This could be called the family without a core. Everyone's behavior is regarded as irrelevant except to himself or herself. Nothing really matters. People come and go without acknowledgment and without explicit expression of meaning to one another. Agreements are kept or not kept at random.

These are the extreme of disorganized family systems. There is no accountability because there is no expectation and little cohesion or relationship developed. These families seem to be the result of situationally and structurally overwhelming stresses over a long period of time, even generations of time, and limited capacity to absorb the stress. As family therapists we meet these families only briefly when they're under a specific stress or requirement of the court or within the structure imposed by an institution such as school, hospital, or correctional facility. The shame of people in these families is related to the lack of development of a self. A basic premise is an individual assumption that "I'm not as good as other people." "I'm irrelevant as a person." "I'm not a part of the larger whole of my group, community, etc." "My promises don't matter and my behavior doesn't really affect anyone else."

The experience of relationship in the respectful system is one of ongoing dialogue over time and of reliability and constancy. The fact that every person is different is more adequately incorporated into the respectful system, as is the fact that every person will make mistakes. It is not possible to be in a close relationship with a person and never hurt that person. We all have our blind spots and our dark sides. Misunderstandings are part of the process of relationships. When these come up in the primarily respectful system, they are regarded as a problem to be dealt with and are resolved as part of the ongoing dialogue. We can describe it as a system with a long-term commitment to work through and resolve at an honest level whatever comes up. This does not mean that the dialogue is never intense or angry. True relationship dialogue includes those feelings "from the gut." What it means is a mutual commitment to take in and respond honestly without threats to break off the exchange or the relationship.

There is a relatively stable level of emotional contact and accessibility within relationships. That means that if husband and wife have close warm rapport today, they can expect a follow-through in their relationship tomorrow. If they have a crisis today, it doesn't mysteriously disappear by tomorrow simply by a change in moods. There will be continuity, a process of dialogue, resolution and repair. People in this family expect to have a sense of process flowing from one moment in the relationship to another and this provides a personal feeling of reliability.

The experience of relationship in the shame-bound system is one of repeated rejection, abandonment and punishment or threats of them, sometimes alternating with feelings of intense contact. A common denominator of relationships in the shame-bound system is that they don't seem to make sense. There is often a missing thread of continuity or flow of emotion and give and take. This failure to make sense is usually more apparent to an outsider than to a member of the system. System members are likely to have accommodated to the nonsensical process and not see it. They accommodate through shaming themselves with messages like, "If I were smarter I'd understand," or "I must be crazy to feel upset about this," or they accommodate through a simple failure to expect continuity in relationships. It never was there and it isn't expected. Some people accommodate through more grandiose or elaborate explanation: "I'm the stronger one so I have to accept her immaturity," or "He may be violent when he's angry but underneath he's got a soft heart," or "He may say vicious things but you have to understand he doesn't mean what he says."

There is little sense of security in this system. In some shame-bound families there are moments of wonderful contact and sharing. This can be the high end of the mood swings in the family and it can be what keeps the relationships together, brief or infrequent as these moments are. But these times of contact, while they feel good and nourish the family in a sense, do not develop a feeling of security in people because they can vanish as quickly as they come. On one day the family can be in extreme crisis. Family therapists get crisis calls those days and there is a sense of extreme urgency that arises from the crisis. Yet the sense of discontinuity in the system is demonstrated by these families when they next appear for an appointment and there is little or no acknowledgment that at the time of the telephone call the very existence of the family was in doubt or that some other extreme threat was imminent.

We received one such call from a mother one day when her adolescent daughter had left home saying she wasn't coming back. There had been an angry episode in which the step-father had grounded her. After consulting on the telephone about alternatives for this distraught mother to deal with the situation, we agreed to keep the family session appointment scheduled for three days later. When the whole family appeared for the appointment and seemed quite calm, we asked what the process had been which brought them from crisis to relative peace. That kind of process question did not make sense in this family. The therapist was regarded as absurd or "picky" for pursuing the question about a now irrelevant crisis. "Oh that! Well, I guess we all just cooled off." There was no resolution and no feeling of flow from one moment to the next.

Because of this quality these families are often called "crisis-oriented." We do not see them as necessarily motivated to have the crises (although that may sometimes be true) but as being chaotic and lacking the control to avoid extremes. The resultant individual stress within these families is very high.

CONTRASTS FROM THE INDIVIDUAL PERSPECTIVE

We discern four distinctions between the two types of systems, based on the personal development of individual family members.

1) Accountability, repair, and resolution versus more shame, despair, and discouragement

The system oriented toward respect produces people who stand accountable for themselves and their behavior. Its members live in an intimate network in which generally they can expect wrongs to be repaired, differences to have resolution, and relationships to have a sense of continuity. Children growing up in this system have the security of knowing there will be continuity through stress, and that allows them to take risks and make mistakes. The adults don't have to "walk on eggshells" to maintain their relationships.

Shame begets shame. Within the shame-dominated system any experience is likely to be interpreted in such a way that it undermines the person and creates more shame. It is a cancer that grows from feeling bad about oneself to interpreting neutral or impersonal experiences in personally depreciating ways. "I should have known that when I really needed white raisins the store would be out of them." "I can't tell anyone about the pain in my knee because they'll laugh at me for falling."

We observe a process which we call meta-shame, i.e., shame about shame, which buries one's self-awareness even more deeply. Perhaps there is an assumption that people *should* feel good about themselves, or that "good" people feel good about themselves or "normal" people do. "Being in pain about myself is a signal that I'm not like others or not acceptable. Now I have to hide the fact that I don't feel acceptable." This shame about being ashamed increases one's sense of alienation and the person moves in the direction of denying more feelings.

As a person disowns more of the self, denies more of her or his own feelings, one tends to project the disowned parts onto other other people (Becker, 1973). Parents see unrealistically positive qualities in their children, spouses make inappropriate interpretations of their mate's behavior, family members develop unreasonable expectations and dependencies in order to fill the gap created by their own denial and self diminution.

As this process continues, other people within the network are affected by the confusing messages. A child takes on the parental projection that he or she is more special than other people, which becomes the seed for feeling alienated and unlike others. A spouse feels the burden of repeatedly disappointing his or her mate's demands for perfection or secure dependency gratification and secretly asks, "What's wrong with me?" Threats to abandon and real rejections and abandonments through the "silent treatment" and relationship cutoffs become commonplace. This tendency of the shaming process to draw a system into a progressively intensifying whirlpool is what we mean by the phrase, "shame begets shame."

2) Deepening and modification of values
through life experience versus
increasing rigidity

As individuals live within the respectful system, there is support for their ongoing maturation as human beings. They take in life experience, make mistakes, and learn from them. Values are integrated not for the purpose of condemning people but for guiding behavior and experiencing personal integrity or wholeness. These values are developed and modified over time. Some become more deeply held and some more lightly as experience is accumulated over years. Within the respectful system individuals are free to continue to learn and grow. They didn't start out assuming perfection and they continue to live in the insecurity of not having a claim on absolute truth. Making peace with that insecurity or at least accommodating to it carries the benefit that people can continue to learn.

Some of the most discontented clients we have known have been people who have never learned how to put themselves into a learning relationship to their life experience or to another human being. To be vulnerable to new learning, to receive something from another, somehow seems to feel so insecure or touches such a sensitive shame nerve that it cannot be tolerated. One example of this kind of person is the intellectualizer who cannot rely on a therapeutic relationship because it feels degrading.

One outcome of the shame-bound system is a rigidity of values. Since experience tends to advance and deepen shame for the members of the system, there is little freedom to interpret the gray areas of life experience in an individual or creative way. Anything unique to oneself or creative is more vulnerable and avoided. People abide by the letter of the law and don't know or sense the spirit of the law.

In a recent case of child sexual abuse the county attorney reported her conversation with the accused mother. The mother had decided to tell the attorney the whole story of her behavior and she described in graphic detail the genital stimulation and contact she engaged in with her children. "Sex with children is beautiful," she said, and she could feel no guilt about such a "wonderful experience." She felt guilty about something else that was hard for her to talk about, she said. It was the fact that she had had an affair with her husband's brother and the reason she felt guilty was that this was against the Ten Commandments.

This is a clear example of the rigidity of the value structure in a shame-bound family. It is well-known among therapists of abusive families that this family system is commonly drawn to the dogmatism of fundamentalist religion. The key factor we are underscoring is the family's distortion of rules and guides for living into inflexible, inhumane judgments. Their laws are applied ritualistically and out of context with the rest of life. The people involved get hurt to preserve the principles.

*3) Greater empathy in personal
relationships versus alienation
and distant relationships*

As individuals accumulate life experience in a respectful system they learn more about what it is to be a human being. This includes a maturing sense of humility—the feeling that "I am one among many." It is said that the wise person knows how little he or she knows. An open person in a respectful system errs. Sometimes the error may be a painful misjudgment or a lapse in one's guidelines for how to be. Within the respectful system a person accepts the fact that she or he has weaknesses. No person is strong in all ways. As we experience our own mistakes and accept them, we become more tolerant of others. Thus our capacity to empathize with others grows and deepens. Being a human being is a constantly unfolding mystery and accepting that in ourselves opens us to feel closer to our loved ones and to learn from their experience.

On the contrary, persons in the shame-bound system do not accept their own incompleteness. They judge themselves for it, and try to deny or ignore it. In a family session with a very shameful client, Virginia Satir commented, "You seem to think you should have been born fully clothed, walking around and talking with a full vocabulary!" In this rejection of their own incompleteness, people don't develop their capacity to put themselves in the place of the other. Thus, the victims of shame become effective perpetrators and perpetuators of it.

With all the differences between the perfectionistic family and the laissez-faire family (Constantine, 1983), we discern some similar emotional impact on the members. Either way there is a failure to support or guide the members into a real involvement with one another and what it is to be a person. In the perfectionistic system there is no forgiveness. In the laissez-faire system there is no accountability. Either way the human process of acknowledging one's limitations honestly and accepting them is incomplete. The impact is to stifle intimacy in relationships. If one cannot frankly see and accept limitations in oneself, one cannot do it with others.

What we find is people in shame-bound systems feeling cut-off, looking for closeness but feeling frustrated, lonely and alienated. Bowen (1978) uses the term "emotional cut-off" to refer to those family relationships in which people have ceased to engage in emotional dialogue. Brothers and sisters in adulthood may go for months or years never validating their relationship by communicating anything real about their lives. Adult children move thousands of miles from their parents and say, "That family isn't relevant to my life today." When they do get together perhaps they talk about sports or the children. In these cut-off relationships they have ceased to exchange meaningful communication about the real experience of their lives.

Sometimes a cut-off takes place abruptly and in anger or

hurt. Sometimes it evolves quietly without acknowledgment that it has occurred. As the ongoing dialogue of primary relationships ceases, the potential for shame to grow in the gap increases. As an index of how embedded in shame a client is, we sometimes ask him or her to count up how many formerly significant relationships they have which are now cut-off. Family therapy with adult clients often includes the revitalization of relationships between them and their parents and siblings. This means establishing a new open-ended dialogue about real life experiences. Sometimes this includes bringing all the original family into therapy temporarily; sometimes it means clients' making visits to family with specific plans to open up the relationship.

4) Growth of self as a whole person
versus development of an image
and control of self

The person in the respectful system is free to grow in ways that evolve from his or her context, increasing in awareness of what it is to be a person. This person has an increasing knowledge and respect for the dilemmas, pains and surprises of being human.

The contrasting position of the person in the shame-bound system does not engage with the experience of maturation into full personhood. This person is seemingly stuck at a developmental level which focuses on outside appearances. "How do I look to others?" "What will the neighbors think?" "How can I conform to the rules?" "How can I sneak by the rules while secretly taking what I want?" "If I could be like that person I would be happy."

This system produces some people who have enormous stubborn strength to control their own behavior or to control the behavior of others. Rather than people in the system growing in their own sense of personhood, they progress toward a cycle of control and addiction. They become more polished and effective in their control, manipulation and outward focus, become less aware of their own personal experience, and lapse more often and more intensely into ritualized, stereotyped, or compulsive behavior.

References

Becker, E. (1973). *The denial of death*. New York: Free Press.
Bowen, M. (1978). *Family therapy in clinical practice*. New York: Jason Aronson.
Constantine, L. L. (November 4, 1983). Private Workshop. St. Paul, MN.
March, W. (1967). *The bad seed*. New York: Dell.
Minuchin, S., Rossman, B. L., & Baker, L (1978). *Psychosomatic families*. Cambridge, MA: Harvard University Press.
Satir, V. (1972). *People making*. Palo Alto: Science and Behavior Books.

3

THE ORIGINS AND PERPETUATION OF SHAME

Shame presents itself in a wide range of affective states; facing shame means facing feelings. But often genuine feelings are not available—due to defenses or repression or denial. When we meet shame, we recognize that we often are meeting the masking of affect, and realize that we need to get behind the mask to find the person. We have discovered that we can enhance this process of unmasking by understanding the origins or etiology of the person's or family's shame. We do this by unveiling the history of the family, searching out the shaming events in particular, to develop empathy for a sometimes "unlikable" persona.

Of therapeutic value to the clients is the discovery that their coping behavior was learned in the family, and that they are not the "cause" of the shame-bound interactional patterns that have resulted in interpersonal cut-offs. They are separate from the shaming events. By naming the shaming events, the clients come to see that as young children in shame-bound systems they had little power to determine how they would interact with the world.

Sharon entered therapy upset about her uncomfortable feelings when with her family. She had recently moved back to her home town and was attempting to reconnect with her family. She complained that her parents' marriage looked dismal and she felt empty when she tried to connect with them. She stated she had felt split off from them since she had started college. During her years away she had engaged in a series of relationships with users and abusers of people; she was victimized and was treated like an object. Sharon could not think of any abuse in her family history and felt troubled about what was "wrong" with her. Currently she was not involved with any intimate relationships, and she didn't have much hope for the future. Her attempt at a "geographical cure" had been of no avail; she still had to face her unfinished business. And her staying away had been serving to maintain the system's secrets.

Whenever she spoke about her family she was flooded emotionally and appeared to be out of control in her sobbing. This terrified her since she had not cried since early childhood. During our search into her family's dynamics, she discovered that her family harbored many secrets and embraced a loyalty to the "let's pretend" quality of the high-achieving family. The members of this high-achieving family had coped with their pain by acting out the attitude, "We will make this family better; *we will have worth!*"

In her family-of-origin sessions, where she presented herself to her family and talked openly about her reality of growing up there, she learned that her grandfather had abused her mother and that all had silently sworn themselves to secrecy. Other secrets, including her father's and brother's suicide attempts, also surfaced during the same session. The client's brother told his father that he had been frightened by his dad's late-night telephone calls in which dad talked about his attempted suicide. Sharon's brother, Dave, felt overwhelmed and confused. He had not known what to do, since dad had told him that his mother did not know anything about it.

As the family secrets tumbled out, the family members sat frozen in their shame. Sharon could clearly see how the loyalty to the no-talk rule had resulted in an affective inheritance that deeply affected her. The unexpressed pain had accumulated through the years and was experienced by her as a sponge-like reaction in which she absorbed and released the family's repressed affect. That which had not been allowed had been passed on, despite all the family's attempts to control it away. As Sharon gradually came to see the connection between her affective pain and the family's repression, she was able to gain a cognitive understanding of her "no fault" inheritance, that she had not developed this alone. Of course we assured her that there was a way out – through breaking family rules and commenting on reality, expressing feelings and talking with family members about her own reality.

Sharon had been loyal to her family's rule about blocking pain by strengthening the cognitive self and coping through intellectual achievements. This blocking did not look like repression; it took the form of containment. The family's collective mask could be described as one of "apparent good health." Underneath it, however, were layers of shame and pain tightly wrapped in denial.

Sharon's story shows the three distinct elements of the origin and perpetuation of shame: 1) the external shaming events (abuse and suicide attempts); 2) the inherited generational shame, passed on to family members (mother's artificiality, dad's rigidity) when the shaming events and the feelings they invoked were denied; and 3) the maintained shame, which Sharon kept alive in her personal and interpersonal world (in her setups to be victimized). Until Sharon faced and openly addressed this shame, she could not be free to become a self-accepting human being.

We examined the etiology of Sharon's shame by returning to her family of origin to learn as much as possible about its history – those events that caused her shame. This cognitive restructuring of the elements of shame is primary to the therapeutic process, so the client, in knowing the reality underlying the family myths, can have the understanding necessary for change. Sharon realized that she was a part of a whole family, that she was a "family fragment" (Whitaker, 1979) carrying her share of the family's pain and strength.

EXTERNAL OR TRAUMATIC SHAME

External or traumatic shame results when a person's body, thoughts or feelings are invaded in such a way that the person feels like, and is subsequently treated like, an object or a thing. When family members give histories, we ask them to list those events in their lives that they consider to have been traumatic. Some adults remember a rather ordinary event, such as hospital care, as physical invasion at a time when they, as children, felt powerless. Often the giving of an enema, the changing of a dressing, or any other invasive medical technique done without warning or permission has resulted in a deep inner knowing that one felt "entered into" in a painful way.

Another cause of external shame is sexualized touch. Children so victimized sense a sexual energy that frightens them, even though the words and behaviors in themselves are not sexual. Many children have been the victims of sexualized affection, which they describe in their terms as "uncle's icky grabbing" or "aunty's smothering kisses." In these cases, the children did not know they were the recipients of someone's sexual neediness and resulting intrusiveness. In fact, unknowing parents have often pushed children toward their relatives, not heeding children's nonverbal cues of "no." These acts further confound their children. Such scenarios are, of course, the birthplace of the shutting down of a child's feelings to accommodate those of a big person (Miller, 1981).

The clearest example of external shame is incest. The victim knows the source of the shame; she knows the perpetrator is a member of the immediate or extended family and, because of the family loyalty, represses or denies the event. She is quite confused about the meaning of a loving relationship and what respect means in relationships. Today we know of the high incidence of incest in families (Meiselman, 1978). What is not acknowledged is the rippling effect of the shaming event—the pervasive shame that affects all family members and the loyalty to the secret. In the victim's shame, she also takes on the burden of feeling responsible for her parents' marriage, fearful that if her "secret" is disclosed her parents will divorce and the family split apart.

Not all external shaming events involve expressions of apparent affection, however. Rape is traumatic as an external forceful assault. The highest percentages (60%) of rapes are classified as "intrafamilial" or "acquaintance"—rape in which the perpetrator is not a stranger to the victim and these figures have increased every year of the 1980s (Chester, 1985). When one adds to this the high incidence of marital rape, the number of women and children suffering rape is staggering (Russell, 1984). Many women think that they are "to blame" for the rape and feel ashamed of themselves for "allowing" it to happen. Many women have stated, "Well, if only I had not worn that silk dress . . . ," accepting a commonly held myth that they are responsible for men's sexual violence. By taking on the shame of the rape, a woman internalizes and maintains her shame, often in secrecy.

Still another type of invasion involves a seductive parent who invades a child's personal space with inappropriate nudity. Allan reported his confusion when, as an adolescent, his mother, dressed in a filmy nightgown, sat talking with him every night about her personal life with his father and hugged him and kissed him moistly on the lips. To a teenager struggling with his sexual identity, and loyal to his mother's "caring," her message was understandably confusing. She loved him but loving in this case meant sexual loving and invasion. He did not know he could say "no" to his mother and found that at age 33 he was still held to his mother by this powerful invisible bond.

The most common clinical presentation of this type of invasion is confusion and terror concerning intimacy in relationships. Allan was able to have close relationships with young women up to a point and then he became frozen in terror. He did not realize that he was bound by a solid but invisible thread to his mother; he had become the caretaker of her heart needs. At a very deep level he seemed to know that if he were to pair with a woman, he would have to sever the tie with mother – the tie holding them both together. Allan worked long and hard to untie this knot, indeed to sever the dysfunctional bond. He then felt free to love on a peer level; he also enjoyed his new relationship with his mother.

When clients do not understand the internal network of shame recorded in their history, with its connecting link to family secrets, a mysterious minefield of shame can be tapped

by a single encounter. The resulting affective response seems
to be exaggerated. A friend might, in conversation, refer to
some event that taps repressed and shame-holding history
in another. The shame-bound person reacts strongly and often
does not know why, leaving both people stuck in a confusing muddle. The responses often seem to be disproportionate
to the event. These awkward situations break the interpersonal connection, with neither party knowing a way out.

Often these strong reactions are born out of projections
from the past. For example, a young professional woman
named Janice had been invaded by her parents in a number
of ways. The only child in an enmeshed marriage, she had
been used by both parents to satisfy their emotional and
physical needs. Both had "helped" her with her toilet, both
walking into the bathroom when she was on the toilet, both
often wiping her after her bowel movements, and mother
often giving her enemas as well. She became the "thing" with
which they filled their intimacy vacuum. Janice repressed
most of this early history; the scenes surfaced only after she
viewed an educational film on childhood development.

When Janice entered group therapy she was very reactive
to anyone's touching her in any way. If someone merely gently laid a hand on her shoulder, she found herself resentful,
rageful, and on the edge of physical aggressiveness. (One of
her repressed memories was of beating up both her parents
when she was 11.) It was evident to others that she feared
any touch; touch was a trigger for her history of shaming,
sexualized, inappropriate touch. She never knew when this
network of shame would be triggered; this led to her wanting
to stay in control. Until she sought therapy, she had thought
her behavior normal. Indeed, it is normal to defend oneself,
but she was expressing anger toward the world which she
needed to direct toward her parents, and because of her emotional reactiveness as she was alienating herself from others
as well as herself.

We saw another form of shaming in a pseudomutual family
in which the "nice guy" dad wanted to keep everything "nice"
at all costs. No one in his family knew what his pain had been;

he was quite comfortably plastic and apparently determined to stay that way. So when his son came into therapy with his feelings of fear and confusion after being attacked in his college fraternity house (he had been pulled out of a window in his sleep, beaten severely, and dragged back through the window), he felt alone with the story because his parents had invalidated his experience. His dad had said, "Now, you know that some bad things can happen to people. Do you need some new clothes for spring quarter?" All of this was said in about one minute – that is all the attention the client received from his dad. His mother sat silently, with a pained expression.

The client's cry of anguish was filled with pain and anger; yet neither parent appeared to hear him. He did receive support and medical attention at school, and his mother had driven down to the campus to talk to school officials. When he returned home, however, it was as if the incident had never happened. The message was: "No pain allowed here, so let's pretend it never happened." Until he entered therapy, he had taken the pain on and felt ashamed for having caused his parents such concern. In therapy he was able to get a reality check and the validation that he had been abused *twice* – first in the college incident and a second time in the invalidation by his parents.

Often post-traumatic syndromes are inherently shame-maintaining. One recent example involves the survivors and returnees from Vietnam. Many veterans were shamed in public and private worlds about their participation in such a war. Many of these men, as well as nurses and other medical personnel (Van Devanter & Morgan, 1983), did not know where to take their recollections of some of the terror they faced there. It took several years for the American public to fully understand the impact of combat on these men and women.

Some of these veterans have experienced this shame constantly. Robert Bly (1985) reports the stories from some physicians in Texas who studied the dream patterns of some returning veterans. He said they discovered that some men reported that their dreams replayed the actual terror they had met during the day's combat, leaving them with no relief from the constant pressures of combat. The shame dynamic presented itself through the shutting down of feelings, a hardening to the pain of terror. One steely-eyed Vietnam veteran commented on his post-Vietnam attitude toward life. His statement to a group of couples was: "I died in 1967 when all my men were ambushed; now I'm just waiting for the act of it." This man would not feel his shame—or any other feeling. His armor was intact; he could survive. He had struggles with empathy, even regarding his children. If his child fell down, he would tell him, "You'll be okay; be a man and take care of yourself." The father was passing on his defensive identity to his son. When these war veterans work through their shame, they do so slowly and with great fear. Often it is like a river bursting through a dam, running its natural course until all the repressed affect is released. With that comes freedom to go on living.

One World War II survivor entered therapy with his family; his wife and daughters were challenging him to let them know him. At one point in the second interview, he stated that he was filled with fear and had been having nightmares recently. He had been the single survivor from his company; his memories of combat were returning and he was terrified. He held his jaw firmly as he stated, "I decided then never to care again." Now he was struggling to keep that commitment.

INHERITED GENERATIONAL SHAME

What types of families are inheritors of shame? The most likely candidates are those that protect their history with secrets, mysteries, and myths.

Stories of inherited shame uncover poverty resulting from bankruptcies, suicides, childhood deaths and accidents where the parents feel they were to blame (or were being punished), or secrets surrounding pregnancies, births, and adoptions. The rules of shame-based systems produce several generations of repressed affect. The family members often feel they individually have inherited some kind of "curse" and have

anxiety and fears, even phobias, about breaking the powerful no-talk rule insulating the shame.

Clinicians can identify inherited shame by working with
individuals in the context of their families. Often the defenses
are such that clients may present themselves as high-achieving, competent individuals with no cares at all; the presenting complaint is an anomaly. This presentation dramatically changes, however, when those individuals are seated in
their families of origin, where they often return to that shame-
filled place in the family. The client's stuckness is clearly seen
in its original context; the clinician can observe the family
rules and coach the client in breaking those rules.

John and Leslie were successful owners of a small business
who entered therapy later in life because they were "sick and
tired" of their marriage; they wanted to improve it or end it.
As part of their therapy both brought in their parents. John,
who had a very calm and mature disposition, became "little"
in the presence of his petite, 84-year-old, white-haired mother.
He turned his toes inward, shrunk down in his chair, and
spoke in a "small" voice. We could see his stuckness, and he
had the necessary support to break the family rules and talk
about issues he had never discussed with his mother. These
were the same issues which had affected his relationship with
his wife, especially his fear of conflict and his resultant dishonesty.

Unresolved grief is another arena for shame. Susan, in a
therapy consultation group with us, was presenting her family genogram to the group and had "x'd" out two preceding
generations who had died in the holocaust. She struggled
with the notion of talking about this with her parents and
also with the thought of having a child. She felt a responsibility to keep the family going, while at the same time she felt
a deep survivor guilt—did she deserve to bear life with all
that the others had lost before her? After participating in a
holocaust family survivors group, she was able to connect
with her parents and sisters in a new way.

What is common to all such families is the commitment
of all family members to maintain the secrets through rigid

rules about what may and may not be talked about. These rules prohibited spontaneity in the family relationships; with spontaneity the real feelings and facts might be revealed.

Family members create powerful myths about their histories, often leaving out the painful historical shapers of the shame. The children in these families are loyal through their lack of questioning about the past, thereby colluding in the family's rules.

Family myths

All families explain the events in their history through family myths. Myths in the shame-bound family are born out of distortions and delusions, and through loyalty function as the barrier reefs to family shame.

A mother of 14 children became sick and died in the 1920s. The father had an incestuous relationship with his daughter and the oldest sister parented the fifteenth child, who did not know that this "older sister" was her real mother. The older sister, Emily, played her role well in protecting the inherited generational shame – to the extent that she chose to play a saintly figure to be held in high regard. She spent her early and middle life giving herself away to others in all kinds of service – caring for an alcoholic husband and "protecting" the children from his violent outbursts, giving to the church in service work, believing that if she were "good enough" God would rescue her. Her son, of course, inherited the "messiah" complex and became a pastor, to his mother's delight. He later married an abused, low-esteem incest victim who bolstered his self-image in exchange for his "rescuing" her. By the time the interactional patterns around the secret had come down three generations, the defensive armor was strong; no affect was revealed in dialogue. The pastor, Eli, who became our client, did not let anyone get too close to him, and his role reinforced this distancing.

As part of some family therapy training, Eli had returned to his family of origin to seek information and had just learned about the incest and his aunt's being his half-sister. He was stunned and puzzled about his mother's disclosure at this time. Even hearing this was not enough; his character armor still protected him. He could recite the history without any sign of feeling connected to it. The pain was well hidden, and in his role he could probably protect that shame for still another generation. Now at least it could be reported as information; family freedom could not surface until the feelings could.

This emotional shutdown over inherited generational shame results in a dynamic similar to that of the chemically dependent family. While we have often referred to the "c.d." family when referring to the chemically dependent family, we referred to this family as the *"other* c.d." family – the *cognitively* dependent family. While the chemically dependent family has chemicals for organizing principles, the "other c.d." family, the cognitively dependent family, has only cognitions (factual, left brain knowledge) for its organizing principles.

MAINTAINED SHAME

Shame lies dormant, waiting to be activated. Shame-bound family members find ways to perpetuate the shame to maintain its place in the system. We have recognized that shame "begets" shame. Shame seeks itself in others in its own magnetic field. For some, loyalty to the shame leads to such strongly established defense structures that the only vulnerability known to the person is the vulnerability of the shame. When feelings are shut down, and when vulnerability is so keenly needed, some people seek whatever mechanism necessary to maintain their vulnerability in some way – that is, they maintain the shame and *some* vulnerability and *some* affective experience, even if negative. The self-contempt experienced in shame is a strong feeling experience, and this affect is functional, maintaining the shame.

Clinically, we see a variety of scenarios resulting from "shame seeking shame." One situation involves George, who engages in serial relationships, sincerely believing that "*this* one is the real one. . . . I now have found what I needed." Out-

siders wonder, "Well, why would someone do such a thing?"
"Isn't it obvious that she is a poor choice for him?" "He knows
that she has abandoned her husband and beats her kids!"

When confronted by friends, George argues rationally
that, together, they are going to do it differently, stating "We
are in control of our lives!" That control is the aspect of their
relationship that can lead to outbursts of either abuse or addiction, maintaining the shame. We asked George to write
out a relationship history, a historical recording of all the
women with whom he had been in short-term relationships;
he listed 82. At a later stage in therapy, he admitted that he
truly believed he was unlovable and that if he let anyone
know him, they would find out what a "schlump" he really was.

In another scenario we saw a family for a "checkup." This
visit was prompted by Mary, who was heavily invested in her
adolescent daughter's weight gain. Ken, the father, said he
was upset too, but could "stay out of it." Mary was concerned
about what might "really" be going on with her daughter and
had been busy buying exercise records, joining dance/exer-
cise classes (inviting her daughter to come along), and making comments to her at the dinner table ("that bread is really fattening, you know"). Of course, she insisted that she was
only being helpful. As Mary spoke, Kathy, her daughter,
assumed a shamed posture—head hanging, silently weeping.
When we questioned her, she stated that she did want to do
something about the weight, but only wanted support, not
management, by her mother. Kathy learned that she "invited"
her mother to "manage" her; she would become passive, withdraw and act sullen, with an engaging helplessness which
Mary felt she couldn't refuse. She reported that she *knew*
Kathy needed help. Kathy learned how to turn to her mother
and tell her, "I'm going to be all right; thanks for the help,
mom." When she learned to befriend herself and act respon-
sibly, she could tell Mary she was not a little girl needing such
monitoring. Her honesty and responsibility convinced Mary
that she had indeed been "fired" from her job of policing her
daughter. At the same time, we talked with Mary and Ken
about the loneliness in their marriage.

These scenarios are reminders that families often become stuck at times of life-cycle shifts with concurrent individual growth issues (entering adolescence). In this scenario, a family life-cycle issue (adolescence with shifting parent-child relationships) bumped up against the daughter's individual growth issue. Staying stuck in this dynamic could maintain the shame, with Mary and Ken feeling like failures and Kathy hating herself for her weight problem.

Another scenario maintaining shame is seen when students (young or adult) are facing examinations of any kind. Shame-bound people with unclear boundaries internalize most outcomes. That is, if they take an examination and fail, they believe *they* are failures. (They would never consider that perhaps it was a poor examination or that they were not prepared for this type of examination.) This reinforces the perfectionism and striving to control in order not to feel the personal failure and maintain the shame.

Learning to separate themselves from outcomes, whether in conversations, relationships or events, takes time and successes. With blurred boundaries, shame-bound people tend to fuse their entire selves with whatever the person or activity is and take all that is outside them very personally by internalizing. A common example is seen in couples therapy when one person comments, "Well, I surely feel better now that there is no more abusive language in our place. It really had me feeling down all the time." His partner interrupted and exclaimed, "There you go again, blaming me for how you felt; I'm sick and tired of your always dumping that on me!" This internalizing is inherent in shame dynamics; a shame-bound person has difficulty seeing that another person is perhaps just making a statement about him or herself. This does not mean that some statements are not manipulative; they are. But the shame-bound person must struggle with listening to others and learn through coaching and experience that when others speak they are making statements about *themselves*. The pattern of self-defeating behaviors — self-hate, rejection, and self-alienation — metastasizes and gradually seems to fill up the whole self, becoming the person's identity. The individual feeds the downward spiral of the cycle of shame through these patterns (see Figure 2).

When the cycle of shame is interrupted, and associated compulsive behaviors faced, people experience a rising self-esteem, the first sign of real hope. They have lived through many attempts at false hope by telling themselves they would not do this again; now, by facing the patterns with the support of others they begin to shed the internalized shame. Gradually shame-bound people are able to look outside and recognize others outside themselves. By making small behavioral changes, discontinuing self-defeating behaviors, people see a way out. One person recently told us, "I wouldn't

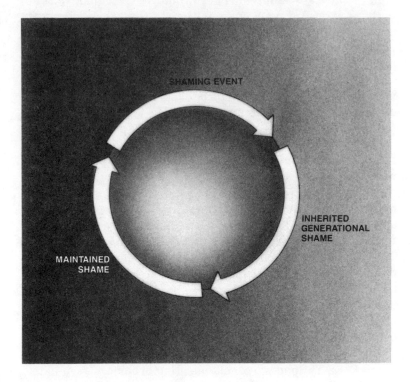

Figure 2 Origin and perpetuation of shame

have shown up there [the office] if I didn't believe there was one little piece of me alive. I had to take the risk." By ceasing the compulsive, anxiety-driven behavior, she was able to begin a recovery process, a process of connecting with herself and with others. She was on the way to becoming a person with high esteem. As her esteem heightened, she could look deeper and learn more about herself.

As clients work more deeply on their closeness issues, we meet some resistance, which we interpret as fear of going where they have not been before. This resistance can be seen in the form of cut-offs. Inherent in the shame dynamic, the interpersonal cut-off feeds the feelings of loneliness and isolation. The cut-off is seen in physical or psychological leaving, and in incomplete transactions with others. Those interacting with the shame-bound person feel abandoned or at least temporarily left. This psychological exit is the loyalty to maintaining the shame by responding to its "split voice."

The split voice of shame comes from the cutting off of the self, the critical self-monitoring voice inside which asks, "I wonder what they think of me," or "I wonder if they'll think I'm dumb." This internal monitoring of all interactions becomes so constant that many people think that it is natural. When people are not able to be present with others, those close to them feel abandoned and shut out. This voice is often masked in a false self, accommodating the shame. This "voice over" sustains the anxiety engine which drives the shame mechanism.

The false selves become safe façades for protecting the shame. Since shame seldom exposes itself in its raw form when clients enter therapy, we initially experience the façades of maintained shame.

THE MYRIAD MASKS OF SHAME

When we face shame, we face the masks and pretenses of a family persona. Families typically cover their shame by adopting a false family self. Individuals don't call for an appointment to say, "I want to deal with my shame and face myself honestly." Rather, what we hear is a voice behind a mask, asking for help. Typically shame is described in terms of low-esteem: emotional shutdown, slumped posture, downcast eyes, blushing, and dulled expression in the eyes. While this is often the appearance of shame, we do not see this initially. To hide the pain of the shame, many people learn to develop masks. There is no one mask; there are myriad masks for shame.

The fairytale family

Some families exhibiting this "let's pretend" quality have taken on a "persona," a family personality that is *apparently* healthy. They have learned to copy behavior from films, from other families, from articles in magazines, from the dominant social myths, and most of all, from the artificial social sets where others play the same game. The game is: "I'll act like you expect me to act in this social situation; I'll conform to the rules. I'll dress appropriately, join the country club, send my kids to private school and participate in the Junior League and other status organizations." In other words, they adopt role behavior that they conveniently assume by accumulating things — for example, they know what cars to drive, what clothing to wear, what meals and wines to serve, what books to read, what vacation spots to choose, what churches to attend.

On the outside, these families are often the envy of others in the community. They live an "act as if" life, that is, they act as if there is a prescribed way for families to live life. By expending such determination and effort on achieving, they can hope to surpass their shame. The message is implicit yet strong: "If you live life by our rules, then all will be well." No one is allowed to tell others outside the family how empty and lonely the family members feel. An inner voice shouts: "Maybe I'll just try harder, and then I'll be like the rest. I cannot let anyone know how inadequate I feel in these roles and these social situations."

There is even a community chant of "Aren't we lucky . . . !"

Happiness is bought, worked for, and external. Accepting this "let's pretend" dimension means walking the fine edge of denial, which serves to alleviate the pain of the secrets. Indeed, they become even more deeply repressed, and the pattern of the game is hyperactivity. If the family members were to stop, they might have to feel the pain. R. D. Laing (1970) describes the rules in *Knots*:

> They are playing a game. They are playing at not playing a game. If I show them I see they are, I shall break the rules and they will punish me. I must play their game of not seeing I see the game. (p. 1)

Sometimes these families become the "forgotten families." High-achieving families are often not allowed by others to have any pain; they look good to all outsiders (and everyone is outside). They contribute to the community and are often elevated and held in high regard. What many in the community do not realize is that if these families were to give up this workaholic pattern, to cease their busy-ness, they would lose their identities as individuals and as a family. Therefore, the parents exert control over the children to achieve, to conform, to pretend, too. If even one child were to escape, all the family's secrets might be spilled – that dad and mom have slept in separate bedrooms for 15 years, that mom's primary intimate relationship is with a woman friend of hers, or that dad often sits alone and drinks too much late at night. Of course, often we see the scapegoat children in therapy; the parents bring them in to be "fixed."

By the time members of these families enter therapy, they often are living behind thick layers of pretending behavior. The persons inside have disappeared. Whatever identity has been formed as individuals, and as family, has become fused with the outer pretending behaviors – that is, the outside self is all that is known. This lack of identity leads to dependency; all are involved in the presentation of the family image. Many younger adults complain that they don't know their parents. The reason they don't is that their parents don't know themselves either. They are giving what they are able to give, what slips out in moments of high stress, for example. These moments or flashes of genuineness or authenticity give the family members hope that if they work at it harder, then there might be hope for more. Couples from these families often enter into therapy in mid-life asking the question, "Is this all there is?"

The disconnected family

Geographical cure characterizes this type of family connection. Often family members have moved away from the home town and will "adopt" a family to replace the family of origin. In essence they have turned away from one another in order to cope with the pain. Some families go so far as to abandon all rituals (birthdays, life marker events like graduations, confirmations, etc.), and often individuals do not know the ages of other family members or their siblings' children. Many relatives become "lost," staying out of touch for decades. Sometimes we see families where half the family is connected and in touch with one another, living a rather close family lifestyle, while the other half is disconnected, not in touch and unavailable except for family crises—and sometimes not then. Adults who have grown up in such families repeat their non-participatory behavior in the next generation, not attending their children's school events, not writing or telephoning other family members, etc. In the clinical setting, at times the most powerful therapeutic event is when the client telephones family members to come into a family therapy session.

Another form of being disconnected occurs in families where roles have been abandoned by the parents and the parents are living as peers with their children. They are, in a sense, disconnected from their appropriate roles. This is different from the family with parentified kids. We have seen examples of this in families where the father has physically and/or psychologically left, and the mother has abandoned her mother role and become a sister to her daughters and sons, with no one truly in charge in the family. Because of the lack of constancy in these families, adult children looking back have difficulty in telling their histories with clarity. They are vague about the family; they are vague about how they feel about it. The children learn to "do life alone," and often pair with someone from an enmeshed family in their adult lives.

Clients from these families are often surprised when they invite their siblings and parents into family-of-origin sessions and receive a positive reply. Often this is a major part of the therapy—taking the risk of asking others to be there for them, with the awareness that the answer may be "no." Family loyalty works powerfully in these families; however, often aging makes a difference, as siblings realize they might be "running out of time" to connect with one another.

The rough and tough family

The mask of toughness is worn firmly in this family. Often the roles are highly stereotypic gender roles, with the macho male and the culturally stereotyped passive female. The rhetoric of the family is the language of toughness—"Get your butt out of that chair and let your mother sit down." The family script is "life is tough; we'll survive it." Family members wearing this mask blame each other as well as everyone outside the family; the rules are those of blame ("his fault," "her fault," but never "my fault"). The rules are clear: It is not all right to be sad, lonely, needing, or tender in this family. This is the mask of survival; the coping has been manifested in putting up multiple fences in order to push back the pain of the shame. The communication style is defended in a shielding armor of harshness and obscenity. The pain is often buried so deep that family members begin to believe that such behavior is normal.

At the end of an intense group therapy session in which several people show vulnerability, one young man from a halfway house for felons asked his friend, "Hey man, do you think we could talk like this when we're with the guys back at the house?" The challenge is immense. Personal growth in these families has been stunted. Like blades of grass shooting up in growth, they have been mowed down time after time, unable to attain healthy growth due to the constant "mowing" of personal assaults.

Shame is ping-ponged back and forth – "I'll shame you first so you can't shame me." This is a vital part of their big-little relationship. It escalates, often erupting in abusive interaction. We often model limit-setting with these families, demonstrating that our rules will be followed – no abuse is allowed in our space. They can swing batakas (stuffed bats for hitting), they can beat on pillows and express all their feelings – but they cannot abuse.

Many of these family members are fearful of their sexuality; they are so frightened of their own feelings of vulnerability and softness or gentleness that they confuse tenderness in a man with homosexuality. They joke about sexuality, make racial and ethnic slurs, and downgrade women. They fear the softness in themselves and suspect it in others.

Often women in these families are dependent on their "men" and, like the men, have been victimized in their early years. The women often seem to be at either end of a continuum – wearing either a mask of hardness and toughness or one of meekness ("he's in charge here"). They allow themselves to be the objects of jokes and sexism and often do not respect women, since they do not respect the woman in themselves.

The nice-nice family

This family mask is characterized by sweet – often sickeningly sweet – affect and smiles, smiles, smiles. Family members often treat one another like children, and sacrifice themselves for one another. One rule is, "If you love me, you will never be in conflict with me." Children often are quite confused because the parents "heap" their love on them by controlling them. The interpersonal language is quite persuasive and always indirect, such as, "You know, Janet's mother told me that Janet goes to church *every* week." The manipulation is covert; requests are seldom direct – they seem bottled in syrup. Anger cannot be expressed openly. Recently when we asked one woman about how she expressed anger toward her parents, she replied immediately, "I married someone they didn't like." One man told us that he never called his mother "mother"; she was called "sweetie" by everyone inside and outside the family. Conformity is born out of this conditional love; often adults do not recognize that this "caring" is exploitation.

Strong religiosity is often a characteristic of these families, with the church used as a rule maker and supporter justifying the "nice" affect in the family. The dynamics consist of so much "giving away" of thoughts and feelings that the person behind the "nice" mask does not have any idea what he or she really thinks about anything or anyone. Individuals from these nice-nice families fear conflict and accommodate others out of their blind loyalty to their families.

The above patterns maintain the shame. The patterns might seem a bit exaggerated, but then, so are the family's dynamics.

One common thread of shame lies behind each mask. Out of the shame-bound rules, with the prevailing control, shame-inducing events are perpetuated and continue the ongoing movement in the cycle — from the inherited shame they have maintained the shame, building the groundwork for the next traumatic shaming events, and contributing another generation's history to the cycle.

When the families can identify their shame and break their rules maintaining it, they are able to take down their masks and express their humanness. They have needed these masks for their survival; we don't take them down until we know why they were put there. The person without defined boundaries has had to substitute a mask for the false self within. These masks, with their accompanying role behaviors, have provided the necessary coping until a person faces shame and develops an identity and boundaries.

References

Bly, R. (January 1985). Jung Society Lecture. Minneapolis.
Chester, B. (1985). Personal communication from Director of Sexual Violence Center, Minneapolis.

Laing, R. D. (1970). *Knots*. New York: Vintage Books.
Miller, A. (1981). *Prisoners of childhood*. New York: Basic Books.
Meiselman, K. (1978). *Incest*. San Francisco: Jossey-Bass.
Russell, D. (1984). *Sexual exploitation*. Beverly Hills: Sage.
Van Devanter, L. & Morgan, C. (1983). *Home before morning: The story of an army nurse in Vietnam*. New York: Beaufort Books.
Whitaker, C. (1979). Personal communication.

4

BOUNDARIES
AND THE SELF

In our early work with boundary confusion, we spoke from our experience with alcoholic or chemically dependent families. We saw dynamics in other families that resulted in our broadening our view. When we presented a workshop at the University of California on "Dependent Family Systems: The Gift in the Crisis," we were somewhat surprised to see an audience from the fields of pediatrics, social work, psychology, school psychology, nursing, *and* family therapy. What these people had in common was their work with schizophrenia, bulimia, anorexia, runaways, as well as chemical dependency.

While much of the literature had been describing the "bulimic family system" or the "schizophrenic family system" or the "runaway family system," clinicians seemed to understand that the basic characteristics of the dependent family system seemed to apply to all. This motivated us to broaden our interpretations, for, just as dependency was common to all, so was family shame. The stories were different and specific to the "type" of family. The family dynamics were *not* very different, however, and seemed to reflect what we were calling the shame-bound system. Specifically, boundary issues were germane to all.

In her early work with the concept of "boundary ambiguity" in her studies of Missing in Action families, family researcher Pauline Boss (1984) discussed the psychological presence remaining when a father was physically absent, resulting in ambiguous boundaries in the family. She defined boundary ambiguity as "a state in which family members are uncertain in their perception about who is in or out of the family and who is performing what roles and tasks within the family system" (p. 536). Finding the parallel in the chemically dependent families, in which we often saw the reversal—*physical presence* and *psychological absence*—we were able to apply the concept of boundary ambiguity to the shame-bound family systems.

We explored boundaries at the family structural level, the intrafamily level, and the intrapsychic level, and saw how each is important to understanding family shame.

FAMILY BOUNDARIES

The *Oxford American Dictionary* defines boundary as "a line that marks a limit." When we speak of family boundaries, we are referring to the invisible line or perimeter, ranging anywhere between rigid or permeable, which sets limits for family members. These limits are enforced by family rules. For example, some families may allow very few to enter, while others have difficulty allowing family members to leave. Some families interact openly with other outside systems; other families avoid such contact. We recognize that there are cultural differences here, but our focus is on how clearly the perimeters are defined.

The development of implicit rule-bound systems governing the movement of insiders and outsiders in family living is common to family life; these are the patterns which are seldom talked about openly but result in well-established behavioral patterns. We can easily see the patterns in the number and frequency of dinner guests (invited or "drop in") a family typically has. Some families' rules indicate "the more the merrier," while other families' rules imply "for members only." Still other families don't seem to have any set rules; it simply doesn't matter who comes and who goes.

Family boundaries have been discussed by many family therapists. Kantor and Lehr (1975) describe the "unit's space," including the thickness of its boundary walls. What they imply is that when one can interact within a unit and count on information about differences and similarities, the unit forms an identity in relation to other units (other families). This family boundary develops from the rules established by the parental subunit, and can change with developmental stages in family life. The clarity of the family boundaries between itself and the rest of society is naturally related to the subsystems.

In their study of "healthy families," the Timberlawn team looked at the family structure. They found no blurred boundaries in healthy families (Lewis, Beavers, Gossett, & Phillips, 1976). Also, Bell (1962) found in his studies of disturbed and well families that weak family boundaries occurred in pathological relationships extending over several generations.

GENERATIONAL BOUNDARIES

Many leading family therapists have written about the importance of clear internal boundaries between the family's subsystems – husband-wife, parent-child and sibling subsystems. Lewis et al. (1976) revealed that a firm parental coalition with no evident competing parent-child coalition contributed to family health.

Minuchin (1974) has focused on rearranging family structure by working with the subsystems, either increasing their boundary permeability or shoring up boundaries. By strengthening the parental coalition (or spouse subsystem), the clinician clarifies the line for the offspring subsystem. Stanton and Todd (1982) have stated that the dysfunctional families of drug addicts have overly permeable generational lines and their treatment program incorporates boundary restructuring and boundary making.

Whitaker (1959) consistently emphasizes the need for a generation gap in families. In support of his strong belief in the importance of clear boundaries, he often brings in the grandparental subsystem to effect change in the parental subsystem. Whitaker discusses the "struggle for territory" and aids spouses in defining and delineating their territories.

In various studies, the following dysfunctional boundary patterns have been noted:

1. Mother-son or father-daughter sexualized relationship (cross-generational boundaries stronger than generational) (White, 1959; Satir, 1967).
2. Seductive child behavior (Morris, 1982).
3. Incompatible marriages, with hostile dependent relationships, in schizophrenic families (Haley, 1959).
4. Anxious attachment and fulfillment of parents' intimacy needs (Bowlby, 1977).
5. Difficulty with separation-individuation (Mahler, 1972).

We have found common threads in reviewing this literature. Dysfunctional marriages with early anxious attachment are the foundations for dependent relationships. While we all project to at least some extent, the children from these marriages tend to find mates who are not clearly visible; they project their idealized fantasy as well as unfinished business on the partner. These children are not free; they are the attachment figures for the parents' intimacy needs and have not experienced the mutual parent-child relationship required during separation-individuation.

The literature review clearly supports our observations that the strength and permeability of the marital boundary directly affects the intrapsychic or ego boundaries of the offspring.

INTRAPSYCHIC (EGO) BOUNDARIES

The infant has no sense of self and nonself during the first few months. Then, gradually, through recognizing where he or she ends and mother begins, the child develops an identity, usually by age three (Mahler, Pine, & Bergman, 1975). When parents are able to give natural caring and it becomes internalized by the child, the "me" becomes separate from the "not me" (Davis & Wallbridge, 1981).

Wilber (1981) stated, " . . . the boundary between self and

not self is the first one we draw and the last one we erase. Of all the boundaries we construct, this one is the primary boundary" (p. 46). He further states that it is difficult to distinguish boundaries *between* things until we have distinguished ourselves *from* things.

Between 18 and 36 months, the child is gradually developing a sense of separateness. When parents have been caught in their own struggles with undefined boundaries, they are emotionally unavailable to recognize and accommodate the child in the drive toward individuation. When a child's separation is facilitated by balanced emotional availability of the parents, the ego boundaries emerge with the differentiation of the self from the rest of the world leading toward identity formation (Polansky, 1982).

Our definition of ego boundary is: *the ego barrier that guards an individual's inner space, the very means he or she employs for screening and interpreting the outside world and for modulating and regulating his or her interactions with that world.* The person who grows up with clear boundaries can mature to a full and competent self; one cannot establish an identity without clearly defined boundaries.

RELATIONSHIP VACUUMS

Many married couples entering therapy have fused boundaries resulting from their undefined individual boundaries. Despite their fusion and high reactivity to one another, the spouses do not feel close. This fusion should not be confused with the strong marital dyad necessary for clear boundaries between parents and children. Many families, especially dependent families, have a prevalence of parent-child "marriages" due to relationship vacuums in the marital dyad.

These parent-child "marriages" are bilateral; that is, when one partner does not love "across" and invests outside the marriage, the other partner finds an outside investment as well. In traditional families, it is not unusual for the father to have his closest relationship with his job or civic work, leaving the affective domain to his wife. Since the husband

is psychologically absent, the woman feels lonely and unfulfilled. She then turns to a child for closeness, pushing the
child into a position that is inappropriate. This child is un-
knowingly trapped, needing to please mom and yet feeling
shameful about usurping dad's spot. Moreover, if dad periodically reclaims his role, the child is pushed and pulled across
the generational boundary, leaving him or her feeling confused and guilty about his position in the family. The dynamic is not gender-bound; either males or females can be
seen as more expressive of feelings.

Children fused to a lonely parent may grow up and marry,
but unless they have "divorced" that parent, the marriage
may well fail. The relationship vacuum will be filled with
drink, or compulsive behavior, or another cross-generational
relationship. The opportunity for mature relationships has
been cut off in each generation.

This issue often presents itself in divorce counseling. Some
family therapists state clearly that they want to make certain the person seeking a divorce is divorcing the "right" partner. The real issues may reside in an earlier generation.

Not long ago Bill, a therapist, came with his wife, Jan, to
talk about divorce. Bill and Jan both complained that there
was no intimacy. We agreed that if, after exploring their marriage, they still wanted divorce, we would work with them
toward their goal. When they were told they would have to
bring their parents in as part of the therapy, Bill was very
reactive, stating that this was "nonsense" and that his mother, especially, would "never understand – she has never even
been in a therapy room!"

With some reluctance, Bill did bring in his parents. In the
session, we asked his mother if she knew why she was there
and if there was anything she wanted from the session. She
said, "I suppose you want me here because of the intimate
relationship I've had with my son all these years and I suppose you want us to get a divorce." She said she had felt guilty about her closeness with Bill.

As soon as we all recovered from our shock at this open

admission, we proceeded to focus on the family of origin and the effects on Bill. Bill talked openly with his mother about what it had been like for him to grow up in his mother's smothering care. He had felt very shameful about his relationship with his mother and felt he had no relationship with his father. Bill and his dad began working on their relationship, as did his mother and dad on theirs. Jan and Bill remained married and recently called to announce the birth of their first child.

Figures 3 and 4 illustrate how in this case a marriage within a vacuum results in generational crossover and boundary invasion. The intimacy vacuum in the parents' marriage resulted in the father's turning compulsively to his work for his closeness and good feelings. His wife crossed the generational line for closeness with her son. Her fear of closeness was accommodated by her husband's psychological absence; she felt more comfortable loving "vertically," that is, loving down rather than across or horizontally. This became the implicit marital contract. The generational crossover formed an invisible parent-child bond and Bill became the unknowing victim in his parents' unconscious plot. *Physical* presence is not enough; *psychological* presence is required for closeness in the family.

Another result of psychological absence is the parentification of children. Bateson (1979) stated that nature tends to fill its vacuums. The vacuum pulls so strongly that there is often a fast adaptation process in a divorcing family, as a child moves up and across the generational line to "pair" with one parent to protect him or her from loneliness and fears. The same is true of the alcoholic family system, where one parent or even both will be psychologically absent and in denial.

Also, the "childification" of the parent can result from the vacuum, as one parent steps down rather than pulling a child up and over the line. Often we hear these parents proudly state, "Why, my daughter is like a sister," or "My son is my best friend."

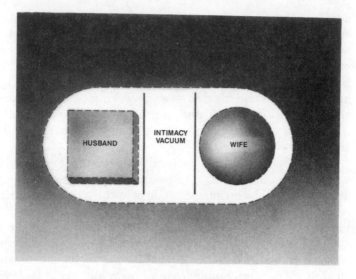

Figure 3 Marital relationship with unclear boundaries

ATTACHMENT

Many adults with undefined boundaries and resulting intimacy struggles have grown up with insecure attachments. It is obvious that children born to an insecure marriage are candidates for attachment concerns. Mahler (1972) states that attachment involves the "caregiver as a secure base from which the infant explores his or her environment." Child development scholars have learned that all infants are attached to primary caregivers, *even if they are punitive.*

Traditionally the primary caregivers have been mothers; feminist therapists are now challenging the child development field about their one-sided approach to attachment. Family researchers are gradually involving the father's role in studying attachment. Of course, adoptions (dual parent and single parent) are also included here. Currently child development scholars are examining the *quality* of attachment, rather than *strength* (Morris, 1982). In his study of attachment between orphaned infants and nurses, Stevens (1982) found that a "spe-

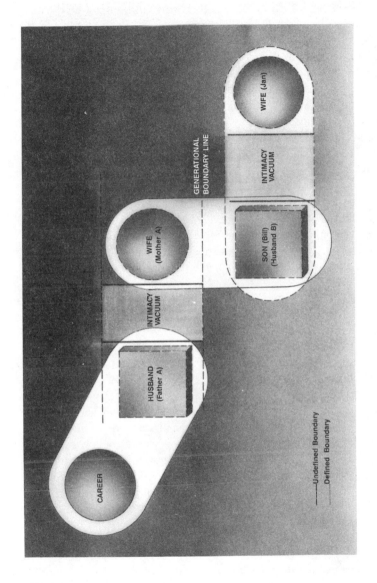

Figure 4 Vertical relationships formed from unclear boundaries

67

cial bond" was formed between a baby and a specific nurse—based on the gradual building of relationship through feeding and caretaking.

Mahler (1972) and Bowlby (1977) contributed greatly to our understanding of attachment. That normal attachment in which the infant and mother form a dual unity or oneness within a common boundary is known as symbiosis. Here we refer to the psychic fusion between infant and mother in which the infant's sense of "I" is not distinct from the "not I." Mahler (1971) calls this the soil from which all other relationships form.

This first attachment, however, is not always successful. No parent can be totally available or present, and a parent's unavailability can be increased by such stressors as depression, rejection, or preoccupation with addictions. Family therapy sessions or family-of-origin interviews seldom fail to reveal myriad life events/stressors preventing or blocking the parent's connecting. The unfulfilled child has become the unfulfilled parent.

Earlier we used the terms psychological absence and presence when referring to parents. Bowlby (1977) used the term "ready accessibility" in juxtaposition to "inaccessibility" when referring to the attachment figures. This means the parent remains accessible and responsive, with the behavior consisting of little more than eye checking. Bowlby states that when young children have this available parent they are free to develop in a natural and safe environment. This also includes the affectional bond, the one-way flow given to the child. It is this reliance upon the nonverbal communication of the caregiver which establishes the child's trust. When this trust is not established, the lack can be well masked.

Recently a couple, Lucy and John, were struggling with their relationship. John and Lucy agreed to participate in a nonverbal exercise together. Each took a turn walking away from the other to indicate how much space each needed in order to feel some separateness from the other. Lucy was able to move across the room and sit alone, feeling comfortable (which raised John's fear of abandonment). When it was John's turn to move away from his wife to "take space," he could only move about two feet, and in direct line so that he could observe his wife's every action. He commented that he did not need to move away to physically get space—he could "leave at any time" (psychologically), thereby remaining in control of himself and in constant observation of Lucy (who felt stifled, angry and smothered). This was a keen reminder to us of the early childhood attachment issues which surface with abandonment and intimacy struggles. His unfinished business with his parents had become his marital burden. His wife blurted out that she was finally understanding how someone could stand very close but at the same time be far away.

Object relations theory stresses the importance of the mutual relationship between mother and child during separation-individuation (Miller, 1981), stressing the effective parenting required for healthy self and object differentiation and integration. The tension bond established when a child cannot move securely from the parent results in a fixed pattern in parent-child transactions governed by strong implicit rules, preventing individuation.

Children who begin with anxious attachment carry on a lifelong search for that secure base. Not clear about where they end and the rest of the world begins, they develop protective mechanisms (defenses) to protect their oversensitivity and vulnerability. Denial and repression become major coping mechanisms for the pain. The message that they are unworthy and unlovable becomes internalized as they continue that script into adult relationships. These adult relationships are naturally dependent, since a secure base is sought in another person. Because the security is not present on the inside, they will always seek this outside themselves. Distortions and delusions will be a part of the perceptual base in mate selection.

Davis and Wallbridge (1981) quote Winnicott's work with "broken boundaries": "distortion in the boundary brings about distortion in the space (and therefore in the maturational processes" (p. 154). These children try to attach to others for a sense of identity and self-worth, forming dependent relationships. It is quite natural to see how the person who cannot get someone to fill his or her needs will turn to other "objects" for fulfillment, feeding anxiety with compulsive addictive behaviors around food, drugs, relationships, etc.

The work of Alice Miller (1981) takes attachment a step further. She states that "the infant's inner sensations form the core of the self." They appear to remain the central crystallization point of the "feeling of self" around which a sense of identity will be established. In her book, *Prisoners of Childhood*, Miller writes about the child who, in an attempt to accommodate needy parents, shuts down emotionally and begins the development of the "false self." When children are able to experience and develop their own emotions, they are able to individuate later. But when children begin to fill the parents' needs and shut down emotionally, they cannot rely on their own emotions and become consciously and then unconsciously dependent on the parents for thoughts and feelings. This dependency is soon transferred to the outside world.

Such was the case of John and Lucy. John's mother and dad had not expressed their very apparent pain over family deaths, and John had learned to protect his parents by foreclosing on his feeling world. Lucy had also given up, since her mother had never talked openly about the pain of her alcoholic marriage or the death of her child at three years.

The insecure attachments, when accompanied by emotional shutdowns, develop into deep feelings of shame and inadequacy.

THE ZIPPER METAPHOR

The zipper metaphor describes the regulator of the boundary or screen encompassing the self. When a shame-bound family has unclear boundaries, and accompanying generational crossovers, the individual's boundaries are very weak or almost non-existent. Figure 5 illustrates the zipper metaphor with the boundary surrounding the intellectual, emotional and physical self and the internal zipper (of self-respect) and the external zipper (of shame).

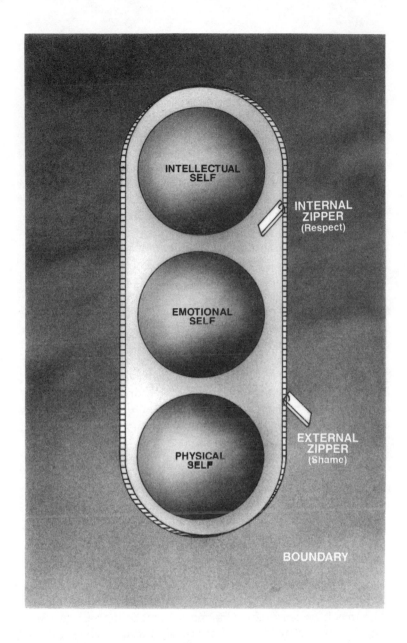

Figure 5 The zipper metaphor

The external zipper (shame)

When individuals grow up in a shame-bound system, they grow up with unclear boundaries, with their zippers on the outside; they believe that they are indeed regulated by others and the outside world.

Rotter (1966, p. 80) states; " . . . boundary can be distorted in itself in the sense of being too weak, or fractured, or even absent when needed." Sometimes this is the result of generational crossover, or of illness, accident, or impoverishment to such a degree that the broken boundary prevents the child from following the natural movement from dependence toward independence. She has learned to feel like an object and allows herself to be treated like a thing instead of a person.

These children (and adult children) are subject to victimization by others, who can come up and unzip them at any time, taking them over and "taking their stuff." These violations result in clients' feeling invaded, yet confused because they feel they have done something wrong to allow someone to "get into my space." The boundary intrusions take many forms, from subtle and not-so-subtle mindreading to parent-child incest. When the boundary is entered, the victim feels paralyzed in shame. Thus, we talk about zipping up and walking away or saying a strong "no."

A characteristic of the external zipper is seen in what can appear to be a lack of common sense. Women or men with undefined boundaries often make poor judgments due to their incomplete interpreting screens, and are harshly judged as "asking for trouble." Undefined boundaries, with denial and repression, prevent clear access to one's sense of what is safe and what is harmful.

These "victims" may not present themselves with stooped shoulders, dragging feet, downcast eyes. Often they appear as quite aggressive, attempting to flaunt independence rather than to acknowledge the deep fear of dependency within. The "aggressive victim" is the apparently boundaryless person who comes charging into the therapy office, literally throws him or herself onto a couch or chair and begins to "fill" the room up with his or her aggressiveness. What is clear here is the strong control the individual is attempting to exert because he or she does not have a *real* sense of self.

Persons with unclear boundaries lack developed identities and therefore walk through life in search of the "other" to fill themselves up. Often one of the clues to the non-person is seen in *highly stereotypic sex-role behaviors* – that is, the ex- aggerated helpless female presentation or the macho tough guy presentation. This "apparent" self or "false" self is the adaptation of a nonself – the person whose innocence was taken too early or the "prisoner of childhood" (Miller, 1981) who became arrested developmentally by shutting down feel- ings to take care of another's needs. In alcoholism studies, we noted that there is less incidence of alcoholism among women and men with androgynous sex-role identities (Rich- ardson, 1981).

Intellectual boundary blurring

Intellectual boundary violations result from parents' in- vading the boundary by criticizing, blaming, mindreading, prying, or mindraping.

Mindreading occurs when a person makes interpretations of another's thoughts and/or feelings without checking them out. Mindreaders assume that they are the experts about what the other person thinks and feels, and that they are *right* about it. The goal of communication is agreement. ("Well, I know how you think about that; you can't fool me.") This is the language of "you" – "You know you just want it to be your way, and you know that the last time you thought that you were wrong, etc." Or it can be couched in sweet rhetoric, "You know you always feel good when you wear that striped shirt, dear, and everyone likes it on you." This example shows how a parent can deny children the right to think and feel for themselves by doing the thinking for them.

It does not take long before a child believes that the big person is right and knows best. When a boundary is violated constantly, there is a good-sized hole in the boundary screen of intellect. The person becomes self-doubting and nontrusting about his or her own perceptions, learning to defer to others.

This is a common form of invasion in many upper-middle-class families. Recently, during a family therapy session, a father was discussing a family issue with his adolescent daughter in a well modulated tone of voice. Gradually the daughter seemed to be shrinking down in her chair. His words seemed gently persuasive and harmless. But to the close observer it was apparent that the dad had entered his daughter's head and was attempting to turn her thoughts into his thoughts. Bach and Wyden (1969) have referred to this as "mindrape." When we confronted this father on his invasive style, he defended himself in an almost self-righteous manner, exclaiming that this was the "only way" in his work and that it was what made him so successful in the business world. Indeed, he had taken his business style into his family living and was upset because it was not working there. This subtly blaming, critical, controlling parent continually reminded his child that she was not quite good enough.

Other parents are not so subtle. These parents openly put down, compare, threaten punishments, etc. They use an army of strong words to belittle the child. Often the child's response is seen in acting out through negative attention-getting behaviors or retreating and withdrawing. Some children become almost invisible, attempting to avoid the barrages. In these families it would be a high risk to express tenderness or caring.

Another form of intellectual invasion is the "prying parent"— the overly interested parent who wants to know *everything* about the child's activities and thoughts and feelings (from the pretense of caring). Often this is a substitute for not knowing how to show genuine concern and accompanies the implicit rule, "If you love me you'll tell me everything." This is typical of the controlling parent whose affective needs and esteem must be filled by the child's behavior. In order for the parent to feel good, the child's behavior must be "good"—thus, the need to pry and keep close control over the behavior.

Often this parental interaction will result in a child's exercising his or her power through holding on to secrets. Tournier (1963) says, "Secrecy is like a strongbox . . . " (p. 20). When shame-bound children live with prying parents, they feel it is their responsibility to give all their "stuff" to the parent in order to be accepted. One father in a family session exclaimed, "Why, my daughter can tell me *everything*! We have long talks at night after her dates with her boyfriend and it's really neat that she trusts me so much. And I can tell her about her mom and me too – we're *that* close!" This unaware and telling disclosure is a clear example of the dynamic which can grow out of unclear boundaries and neediness. And this daughter will probably not realize that she is being exploited until some later time.

Still another form of invasion is "talking over" – the interruptions, the corrections of speech patterns or incorrect word usage, the completion of others' sentences, as well as raising of voices.

Whatever the style of the intellectual violation, one common denominator remains – the children in these families grow up feeling ashamed of themselves. They cannot think or speak for themselves and therefore feel inadequate and inferior. The breaks or violations in the boundaries leave the child victim to others' invasions *outside* the family, leading to the inducement and reactivation of shame.

Emotional boundary blurring

Have you ever been told a secret and then wished you could get rid of it? Or has the knowledge of friend's affair left you feeling uneasy, ashamed? Imagine, then, how a child must feel when a parent shares with that child secrets that should be for the spouse only, especially the parental "secret" of sexual relations. This is emotional rape and has lasting effects on the child.

Lonely, angry parents who cross the generational line to share their personal intimate feelings with their children bind their children to them. This powerful emotional fusion can often be missed in individual therapy. One of the cues to emotional rape is seen in people blaming one parent while defending the other. Or, as Bowen (1979) has stated, "The extent to which you blame is the extent to which you are stuck in your family." It is not unusual to see adults fight to protect the parent to whom they are fused.

Emotional deprivation or psychological abandonment also result in emotional boundary confusion, as well as self-defeating behaviors. The child here has no solid person against which to push him or herself to test personal limits, a requirement for identity formation. The lack of feedback results in a feeling of abandonment and an early life message, "I must do it myself," and "I can only count on me." The underlying message here is, "If I had been a better person, someone might have loved me." Emotionally deprived siblings may fuse, forming a strong emotional union with one another — with dynamics sometimes reflecting the parents' marriage.

Some shame-bound persons are like sponges — soaking up the feelings of others in a room, and taking on the pain of others as if it were their very own. Confused about whose feelings are whose, they are unable to control their affective responses and remain victims to others' feelings. They are set up to pair with someone who has unexpressed pain and will do the feeling work for that person. Many victims go to great lengths to remain loyal to a family rule declaring that one parent is not to be allowed to express his or her own pain. This is the dynamic of dependency and of shame-bound families.

Another example of emotional blurring comes from the expression "emotional anemia," which Horvitz (1982) has described clinically as "the deficiency in the acknowledgment and acceptance of affection, appreciation and closeness from others" (p. 4). Horvitz states that clients commonly isolate themselves from positive recognition, refusing to accept others' appreciation of their good points, competence, skills, and resources. Emotional anemia is another name for shame. The person with shame or "emotional anemia" tends, upon receiving positive comments, not only to reject the comment, but also to mistrust the person as well. Deep down he believes that the person giving the compliment must be wrong or stupid to praise a worthless being.

The person with emotional blurring often grows up seeking emotional highs, living with polarities of intense feeling changes and emotional flatness. He may react to others' statements with strong feeling responses, often feeling ashamed later about sudden, impulsive outbursts of uncontrollably intense reactive feelings. It is another form of giving oneself away by being out of control. Yet he may feel emotionally empty, robbed or drained of affect through his unzipped boundary. Emotions – even his own – are not to be trusted.

Physical boundary blurring

Early physical boundary breaking results from sexual boundary violations (incest) or physical abuse.

Perhaps the most obvious physical boundary invasions clinicians see are incest, battering, and rape, including marital rape. Recent studies of family violence show that approximately 1.4 million children experience acts of abusive violence each year (Gelles & Cornell, 1985). Marital violence has increased in recent years, with reports that one in four couples reported violence at some point in their marriage. Premarital studies show violence also; between 20 and 50 percent of dating couples report experiencing violence (including hitting, punching, kicking, and biting). Henton, Cate, Kovel, Lloyd, and Christopher (1983) reported an especially disturbing finding from their studies: More than one-fourth of the victims interpreted the violent acts as love.

The painful and powerful secrecy of incest often results in intense sexual shame and can lead to the victim's feeling (and sometimes behaving) like a passive, open receptacle. Studies of juvenile and adult prostitutes reveal histories of sexual abuse. The exploitation in the family leaves these women without strong physical boundaries and readied for the invasion or violation by others. With the loss of innocence, we often see an emotional shutdown, with the internal message of, "I am unlovable, and I shall prove it; you will leave me too." This seductive dynamic gives the appearance of the narcissistic personalities who assume that since no one else can be relied on to give loving, they will love themselves.

Sexual shame often grows out of poor body image, childhood family teasing about the body, and shaming bathing experiences. Often clients have reported sleeping with parent(s) and feeling uncomfortable with the "stroking." Other sources of physical shame are physical deformities, being "too short" or "too tall," "too fat" or "too skinny," superfluous hair or lack of hair, scars, casts, etc. While these are not broken boundaries, the shame response results from a heightened sensitivity to others' comments about any aspect of the differentness from the norm.

When children have known physical violations, or at the other extreme, physical withdrawal, they will grow up with discomfort or fear of touch. A recovering chemically dependent woman stated that she did not want to go to her AA meetings anymore because she felt paralyzed in shame when people came up to her and hugged her in friendly greeting. Her group friends did not know that she was an incest victim and was fearful of *any touch*, even friendly, nurturing touch. Because of the diminishing, humiliating experience of shame, she was unable in her frozen state to make any comment to her friends. The result was that her friends' nurturing greetings became her moment of terror.

Female victims of sexual abuse talk about their "freezing" responses to shame. That is, they experience agoraphobia and feel very fearful in any public place. Their "self-consciousness" or "split-self" of shame is so overwhelming they become totally absorbed in their self-monitoring and in their distortion of what other people might think of them.

In this process the self-conscious self observes the other self. It is quite easy to see how a person repeatedly invaded can believe she is a thing, an object to be bartered, used or protected. The cut-off of the feeling world results in their often feeling split in two. Of course, when this occurs, the interpersonal bridge is also broken. Without a foundation of self-respect, these victims cannot zip themselves up. Yet, they try to shield themselves by other means: extreme defensiveness, overweight, and cigarette smoking for example. Still others withdraw socially. All provide a barrier to closeness. In working with male adult sex offenders in a treatment program, we learned that all the men had been deprived of nurturing touch in their childhood experiences. What they had been denied, they had later taken; in the process they ended up violating others' boundaries. The denied or invaded touch resulted in that victim's "taking" safe touch from some vulnerable young person.

Consequences of physical boundary violations are frequently seen in couples seeking sex therapy. Often the past physical invasions (many of which are repressed) have left scars and fears that not necessarily presented with obvious cues. One client remarked candidly, "I know the lights are on in my house, but there's nobody home inside." Here the outer and inner worlds are not congruent; she had learned well how to act "as if," but in the intimacy of her marriage both were discouraged and unfulfilled. It appears that many women and men become emotionally arrested at the time of the physical boundary breaking and many have almost given up hope. For many, sex has become a commodity; a pattern of sex for barter or for power or revenge has developed. Some treat others as well as themselves as objects.

The zipper metaphor is illustrated by Rotter's (1966) work with locus of control. He found that personality types with external locus feel the world to be unpredictable and truly out of any personal control — they feel that destiny is shaped by fate and that there is no connection between their behavior and how their life is taking shape. Many have given up. Focusing on the zipper metaphor allows clients to see that they did not do this alone, that it is multigenerational, interpersonal, and that it can, indeed, change.

The internal zipper (self-respect)

In discussing the internal zipper, we realize that it might sound like we are presenting the prototype for the "ideal" person. We intend here to include what *can* be present in the growth of a healthy person. Typically, normalcy has been assumed to be the absence of pathology, but we have all learned that wellness is much more than that. We hope to provide some dimensions of natural development which also come to us from our clinical practice. To a very real degree we learned about what is normal from what is absent, as well as from what is *present*, in families.

The internal zipper is the regulator for one's boundaries, one's self-respect and integrity. By careful regulation of the internal zipper, a person can be true to his or her own value and be responsible, to the extent that this is possible. Our goal in therapy is to shift the zipper from the outside to the inside.

When children grow up with a secure base, receiving a one-way flow of love and validation for their feeling worlds, they can then begin the development of a self, of an identity. When children have secure attachments, they can make choices and have secrets. (That is, they can have a secretive knowing about their private worlds.) They can begin the pathway to self-respect, individuation, and maturity. These children will be able to express feelings of loneliness, sadness, anger, and hurt. Of course, we recognize that we live on a continuum of the development of self-respect, and all of us face experiences of embarrassment and shame.

Intimacy can come more easily when zippers are on the inside, for when people feel fearful of others, or unsafe, they can zip up and say "stop it" or "I don't feel good about this" or simply walk away. In addition, the capacity for intimacy is great, because with defined and clear boundaries they have identities and an intuitive knowing about where they end and the rest of the world begins. They can monitor the closeness by monitoring their zippers. One needs a sense of control in order to let go of control in intimate relationships. Children can have a sense of the "space" around them and the comfort level and let others know about that. Later, this makes it possible to enter into mature loving relationships, relationships developing from personal affluence rather than from need.

Intellectual boundary building

When one's intellectual self is developed, one can think and speak for one's self; accuracy is more important than agreement in interpersonal communication. This is seen when children can feel safely assertive in expressing opinions and thoughts, wondering out loud and asking questions freely. One can be a curious thinker and explore concepts freely with others. One will grow up freely stating, "I'm wrong, I'm sorry, I made a mistake." This person has an inner knowing about being a human being and will teach others to treat him or her with dignity and respect. This person also knows it is all right to have something private and secret without feeling guilt. This person can stand up for her beliefs even when in a minority.

Emotional boundary building

Persons with an internal zipper know that their good feelings will come from their own behavior. Persons who, in childhood, have been able to express a full range of feelings and feel validated for those feelings will typically enter adulthood with a solid range of affect. They will have an understanding that feelings are neither good or bad; they just *are*. The emotionally mature person is able to choose what feelings to express to others and will have some control over feelings. This person will also be non-blaming and know that his or her feelings are not dependent on others' actions or the cause of others' behaviors and feelings. Of course there are many events and social stimuli which will evoke strong feelings. Children whose affect is developed can experience empathy from their parents when expressing those feelings. They will be able to be vulnerable when feeling safe with others.

In discussing the development of the emotional self, there is an assumption that the child was fortunate enough to be born into a family in which the parents had their own emotional connection and could therefore affirm a child. In writing about affective development, we do not presume that this child does not know shame or has not been shamed. It is not possible in this culture *not* to be shamed in some context. Because one's affective domain is closely linked to values, emotionally mature persons will feel shameful about misdeeds, wrongs, and mistakes, but will be self-forgiving and accepting. They will experience guilt, not shame. They will not be *ashamed* of themselves. That is, the emotionally mature individual knows that there is a dark side as well as a light side in each of us and can accept this self-knowledge. Also, the emotionally mature person can sit with another person in pain and not take the feelings on, but can have empathy and compassion for that person. They know that life has suffering; it is a part of being human.

Ethnicity also influences affective expression. Cultural rules play a major part in emotional expression and these patterns are blindly followed. An 83-year-old Swedish mother who came into a therapy session with her 52-year-old son turned to us and asked, "Do you think it is all right for a mother to tell her son she loves him?" This first-generation immigrant had brought her home country's rules for closeness with her, including one about not stating her caring aloud to her son.

Physical boundary building

Physical boundaries require a clear sense of physical space. Those with defined boundaries can intuit distance comfort and discomfort and can move away or toward someone. They have good sense of esteem about their physical selves. They have grown up with people respectful of their physical space and have had appropriate recognition of their developmental needs regarding modesty and openness.

People growing up with internal physical zippers are congruent, following philosopher Marcel's (1978), "I am my body" (p. 177). The body and the self are one, and their language reflects this. Healthy physical people will grow up to say "I," not "it," when referring to their bodyselves, since they know they are persons ("I"), not objects ("it").

These persons are able to touch and be touched, with, of

course, discrimination. They are able to nurture and receive nurturing. The self-care of the physically mature will be evident in how they care for their physical selves. That is, rather than focusing on the "adornment" of the outside, they show respect for themselves through regular exercise, balanced diet, and self-care. Since the bodyself can be a vivid source of shame, it is important for children to be able to explore themselves with appropriate developmental information from parents.

Persons growing up in a family where sexual development is affirmed will have higher self-esteem than those children who grow up in families where no positive feedback is given regarding their very visible body changes. Children who have physical birth defects can indeed have high esteem relating to their physical selves.

Again, we are reminded of the analogy of the internal zipper to internal locus of control work by Rotter (1966). Rotter found that when people believe they are in control of what happens in life, they can believe that any reward is contingent upon their own behavior and/or personal attributes. In other words, the person with internal locus of control finds the world quite predictable with natural consequences for behavior.

FROM FALSE TO REAL SELF BY FACING SHAME

Through discussing the zipper metaphor, we have talked about the development of the false self of the shame-bound person. The patterns learned in the family of origin have been passed on through strong implicit rules and become the patterns of adult behavior. When individuals can acknowledge and identify shame and understand its roots, they can then face shame as a resource toward individuation and maturity. When emotional deprivation or invasions can be faced and worked through, persons can begin to build an inner self. As boundaries are established, an identity is formed and self-trust increases. They move from self-consciousness to conscientiousness. By facing shame, people can begin the human recovery process, the growing of that budding self within, to a self with respect and integrity, capable of intimacy.

References

Bach, G. & Wyden, P. (1969). *The intimate enemy.* New York: William Morrow.

Bateson, G. (1979). *Mind and nature: A necessary unity.* New York: Dutton.

Bell, N. (1962). Extended family relations of disturbed and well families. *Family Process, I*(2), 175–195.

Bolen, J. (1984). *Goddesses in everywoman.* New York: Harper & Row.

Boss, P. (1984). Family boundary ambiguity: A new variable in family stress theory. *Family Process, 23,* 535–546.

Bowen, M. (October 1979). Family therapy. Paper presented at the Family Therapy Conference, Milwaukee, WI.

Bowlby, J. (1977). The making and breaking of affectional bonds: Etiology and psychopathology in the light of attachment theory. *British Journal of Psychiatry, 130,* 201–210.

Davis, M. & Wallbridge, D. (1981). *Boundary and space.* New York: Brunner/Mazel.

Gelles, R. & Cornell, C. P. (1985). *Intimate violence in families.* Beverly Hills: Sage.

Haley, J. (1959). The family of the schizophrenic: A model system. *Journal of Nervous and Mental Disease, 129,* 357–374.

Henton, J., Cate, R., Kovel, J., Lloyd, S., & Christopher, S. (1983). Romance and violence in dating relationships. *Journal of Family Issues, 4,* 467–482.

Horvitz, A. (1982). Emotional anemia. *Brain/Mind Bulletin, 7*(13), 1–4.

Kantor, D., & Lehr, W. (1975). *Inside the family.* San Francisco: Jossey-Bass.

Lewis, J. M., Beavers, W. R., Gossett, J. T. & Phillips, V. A. (1976). *No single thread.* New York: Brunner/Mazel.

Loevinger, J. (1976). *Ego development.* San Francisco: Jossey-Bass.

Mahler, M. S. (1971). A study of the separation-individuation process and its possible application to borderline phenomena in the psychoanalytic situation. *The psychoanalytic study of the child. 26,* 403–424.

Mahler, J. S. (1972). On the first three subphases of the separation-individuation process. *International Journal of Psycho-Analysis, 53,* 333–338.

Mahler, M. S., Pine, F. & Bergman, A. (1975). *The psychological birth of the human infant.* New York: Basic Books.

Marcel, C. (1978). *Homo viator*. Gloucester, MA: Peter Smith.

Miller, A. (1981) *Prisoners of childhood*. New York: Basic Books.

Minuchin, S. (1974). *Families and family therapy*. Cambridge, MA.: Harvard University Press.

Morris, D. (1982). Attachment and intimacy. In M. Fisher & G. Strickler (Eds.). *Intimacy* (pp. 303-317). New York: Plenum Press.

Polansky, N. A. (1982). *Integrated egopsychology*. New York: Aldine.

Richardson, A. (1981). Androgyny: How it affects drinking practices: A comparison of female and male alcoholics. *Focus on Women: Journal of Addictions and Health*, 2,(2), 116-131.

Rotter, J. B. (1966). Generalized expectancies for internal versus external controls for reinforcement. *Psychological Monographs*, 80 (1).

Satir, V. (1967). *Conjoint family therapy*. Palo Alto: Science and Behavior Books.

Stanton, M. D. & Todd, T. (1982). *The family therapy of drug abuse and addiction*. New York: Guilford.

Stevens, A. (1982). *Archetypes: A natural history of the self*. New York: Morrow.

Tournier, P. (1963). *Secrets*. Atlanta: John Knox Press.

Whitaker, C. A. (1959). Process techniques of family therapy. *Interaction I*, 4-19.

White, R. W. (1959). Motivation reconsidered: The concept of competence. *Psychological Review, 66*, 197-333.

Wilber, K. (1981). *No boundary*. Boulder: Shambala.

5

FAMILY RULES OF
SHAME-BOUND SYSTEMS

The idea of "family rules" is used to describe repeated patterns of interaction that family therapists notice in a family. These rules are descriptive metaphors (Jackson, 1965), unlike the rules and regulations that are decided on by authority. Therapists deduce them *after* noticing patterns of interaction in a given family. Family rules are descriptive of the forces working within the family which influence behavior. The eight rules which follow represent a recurrent pattern of rules we have seen emerge as characteristic of a shame-bound system.

1) *Control.* Be in control of all behavior and interaction.
2) *Perfection.* Always be "right." Do the "right" thing (Ford & Herrick, 1974).
3) *Blame.* If something doesn't happen as you planned, blame someone (self or other) (Ford & Herrick, 1974).
4) *Denial.* Deny feelings, especially the negative or vulnerable ones like anxiety, fear, loneliness, grief, rejection, need.
5) *Unreliability.* Don't expect reliability or constancy in relationships. Watch for the unpredictable.
6) *Incompleteness.* Don't bring transactions to completion or resolution.
7) *No talk.* Don't talk openly and directly about shameful, abusive or compulsive behavior.

8) *Disqualification.* When disrespectful, shameful, abusive or compulsive behavior occurs, disqualify it, deny it, or disguise it.

These eight rules for interaction would serve as effective guidelines for developing a dehumanizing, shame-bound regime in any human system, whether a nuclear family, a staff work group, a corporation, a medical school or an elementary classroom. The interaction flowing from these rules insidiously nullifies or voids one's experience as a person. Relationships in the system don't support a sense of personhood; rather, they undermine the faith that "I am a person" and inhibit the growth of a self-accepting outlook.

This list of rules is not intended to be exhaustive or exclusive for shame-bound systems. It is a working list of recognizable patterns. Another set of observers looking at the same patterns could describe an equally valid set of rules in somewhat different terms. Furthermore, families are different in their way of manifesting these patterns and different in the degree to which they are bound in shame. All families probably have some aspects of shame in their system and we would expect it to show in their rules. The most tightly shame-bound system is easily recognized in these eight rules. Some families strongly emphasize one or two of the rules and do not use others of them at all. The less shame-bound family will have many other more enhancing and humanizing rules, and the shame-oriented rules may appear only under stress.

All humans at some time experience injustice, assault, disqualification, invasion and betrayal. No person is completely shielded. We need not trace out family trees very far back or study for long what life was like for our forebears to uncover humanity's abusiveness. The inherited scars of our multigenerational families exist in our family systems as we know them today. The abuse of the past often exists as the shame of today, and the shame is perpetuated through our patterns of interaction. Let us look at the rules controlling those interactions.

1) CONTROL

Be in control of all behavior and interaction. The control
rule is the cardinal rule of the shame-bound system. All of the
other rules flow from it and support it. In some families the
control principle seems synonymous with a primitive drive
for domination and submission. The satisfaction is in experiencing the power to impose one's will upon others. Furthermore,
when one's personhood is undeveloped and one's repertoire
of relationship skills is very meager, domination-submission
roles provide a primitive formula for getting together with
another person. This meanest form of overt control is usually not passed around from one member of the family to another. It is rigidly held by one or more family members over
the others in a tyrannical manner. Members without power
live in anxious fear of those with power. Yet, it is sadly true
that those without overt power are also loyal to the unjust
system because it provides them, too, with a predictable pattern for relationship and covert power.

Both the tyrant and the victim in the system have a very
limited sense of themselves as persons, inadequate development of relationship skills and no understanding of the nuances of intimacy. Painful as it may be, both of them are
stuck with the roles they know and loyal to those roles until
life experience and learning expand and deepen their repertoire. A therapist cannot assume that everyone has had life
experiences which taught him or her how to be in respectful,
enhancing relationships. We see people in tyrannical systems
who have never learned how to relate beyond dominance and
submission – abuser and victim patterns. For this reason,
brief therapy approaches with the shame-bound family have
limited value. Therapy with this model includes learning the
skills to be in relationships in intimate and respectful ways.
Such learning through evolution of positive relationships
takes time.

Commonly, the control principle is motivated not so much
by a drive to power as by a drive for predictability and safety. Beneath the power-oriented, manipulative behavior we

usually see a frightened person. Spontaneity and surprise are threats within this system and interaction is characterized by manipulation rather than domination. Given the fundamental unpredictability and insecurity of life, when the system is organized around controlling what cannot be controlled, many failures, stresses and distortions of human experience are the side effects. Family members become overspecialized in their control-maintaining styles. One family member may be controlling by sickness, another by being overly helpful, someone else by constant subject changes, another by cuteness and seduction, another by superior competence or super achievement, and another by intellectualizing all experience. The variations are countless.

In this process people aren't truly accountable for their behavior, no matter how "good" it may seem. The indirectness of these controlling techniques in effect puts them out of the reach of accountability. Who can take someone to task for being sick? How can you challenge someone who is only trying to be helpful?

Spontaneous and authentic responses seldom emerge in family interaction following this rule. Behavior to produce a desired response in others or convey an impression are a standard part of all their interaction. We see a family of images, eternal strangers to one another. People hold tenaciously and unconsciously to a narrow range of repetitive responses or games that serve to conceal rather than reveal themselves to each other. After years, everyone in the family knows each other's next lines in the relational dialogue, and yet they remain imprisoned by the patterns. Where communication is heavily loaded with indirect motives, people are constantly focused on mind-reading and discovering each other's intentions. Thus, each person's individual subjectivity stays undeveloped for lack of attention, all attention going to deciphering the messages of others.

Leslie Farber (1976, p. 32) refers to people caught up in this control principle as suffering from a condition of the "disordered will." Most people in these families do not experience themselves as willful or overbearing. They're more likely to

experience themselves as meaning well, or feeling sick, or trying to be helpful, or in some way innocent and congruent with
their values. In their search for predictability and security
they are like the gambler who wins once in a while and cannot quit. What they are not aware of is the powerful and compelling indirect reward they get for their individual willful
ego. The fact of this unawareness protects the silent power
of their willful controlling behavior.

Farber continues:

> This has been called the "Age of Anxiety." Consider-
> ing the attention given the subject by psychology,
> theology, literature, and the pharmaceutical industry,
> not to mention the testimony from our own lives, we
> could fairly well conclude that there is more anxiety
> today, and, moreover, that there is definitely more
> anxiety about anxiety now than there has been in
> previous epochs of history. Nevertheless, I would
> hesitate to characterize this as an "Age of Anxiety,"
> just as I would be loath to call this an "Age of Af-
> fluence," "Coronary Disease," "Mental Health," "Diet-
> ing," "Conformity," or "Sexual Freedom," my reason
> being that none of these labels, whatever fact or truth
> they may involve, goes to the heart of the matter.
> Much as I dislike this game of labels, my preference
> . . . would be to call this the "Age of the Disordered
> Will." It takes only a glance to see a few of the myriad
> varieties of willing what cannot be willed that enslave
> us: we will to sleep, will to read fast, will to have
> simultaneous orgasm, will to be creative and spon-
> taneous, will to enjoy our old age, and, most urgent-
> ly, will to will. If anxiety is more prominent in our
> time, such anxiety is the product of our particular
> modern disability of the will. To this disability, rather
> than to anxiety, I would attribute the ever-increasing
> dependence on drugs affecting all levels of our socie-
> ty. While drugs do offer relief from anxiety, their
> more important task is to offer the illusion of heal-

ing the split between the will and its refractory object. The resulting feeling of wholeness may not be a responsible one, but at least within that wholeness – no matter how willful the drugged state may appear to an outsider – there seems to be, briefly and subjectively, a responsible and vigorous will. This is the reason, I believe, that the addictive possibilities of our age are so enormous. (1976, p. 32)

This control dynamic is being played out intensely and subtly in families with symptoms of psychosomatic and phobic disorders and, as Farber observes, it is a concept relevant to the problems of depression, suicide, drug addiction and sexual problems.

2) PERFECTION

Always be "right". Do the "right" thing. The tyranny of being right can be manifested in many different forms. In one family being right means always knowing and following the latest fashion in clothing, furniture and entertainment. In another family this rule may lead people to "shun materialism and all of its evil ways" and seek a form of self-righteousness found in rule-bound fundamentalist morality. Another family's value system will emphasize intellectual snobbishness rather than moral self-righteousness. In other families being perfect may mean always buying the right consumer item, going to the best school, knowing what is "in," or saying the "right" thing. We are not referring to a morally congruent life nor to a pleasure in knowledge nor a pleasure in being fashionable. Rather, this rule imposes a requirement and a tension on people to comply with a perfect external image, which is sometimes vaguely defined and shifting.

There is always a competitive or comparative aspect to this rule, though it is often denied. Being right never means "right in terms of what fits for me." There is a better-than-others aspect to it or more-right-than-others aspect. People compare and compete with each other inside the family and with others outside the family. The most respected family in the community, when controlled by this rule, may look well put together on the outside while its members are privately suffering with great personal shame.

With the perfectionism rule we often see people anxiously avoiding what they fear is bad, wrong or inferior. It would seem that the fear and avoidance of the negative is a much stronger organizing image in their lives than a simple attraction toward some positive ideal. Such families are living as if the hounds of shame are in hot pursuit. Their system's ethic seems haunted by memories of being badly treated and shamed, perhaps in a previous generation. Suicides, physical deformities, learning disabilities, racist abuses, childhood abandonments, pogroms, orphanage experiences can all be interpreted, on some level, as the victim's own fault. The conclusion within the system is "look good and do or be right" as a protection against shame.

A father in a nuclear family we saw was especially committed to being socially nice and proper, to the point of superficializing his intimate interaction with his wife and children. He had the form of doing what's right, but with little heart. It was easy to understand how this developed when he described growing up in a chaotic family in the suburbs. He was painfully aware in his adolescent years of the social propriety around him, which contrasted with his own home, where his mother was "crazy" and often brought home a new "boyfriend" to spend the night. He said, "I remember wondering how she could talk to a guy with such loving terms as 'dear' and 'honey' when she had just met him that day. Then the kids in the neighborhood would ask me if my mom was a prostitute." It seemed that he had been so shamed in that childhood context that he only knew how to look as good as he had longed to look as a child. Until therapy the substance of authentic relationships was beyond his awareness.

Some systems appear loyal to the perfection rule in a paradoxical way. Their version would say, "Do the right thing in order to be worthwhile," but they have a hopelessness about it or are defeated and demoralized. These systems are chaotic and lacking in standards because there seems to be no point in trying. Following the perfection rule is hopelessly impossible for them, but there is no liberation for them because it is still to be admired in others. They lack the social camouflage of pseudo-propriety that some of their soulmates in shame have available.

The family which overtly emphasizes this rule is the family that embodies all of the stereotyped values held up by popular culture. They are intelligent, high achievers, dressed in accordance with the latest trends, probably athletic, socially gracious, and winners in all externally definable ways. Covertly they are maintaining their shame. What shows is not the problem in this family. Their problems evolve after they fulfill the stereotype of a winner and their models for personhood don't lead them any further. Their relationships have form without soul. The symptoms they bring to a therapist, whether depression, phobia, child behavior problems, or something else, seem puzzling and unrelated to the family system. When the perspective of the perfection principle is applied, it points toward therapeutic interventions which deepen relationships and support authentic interaction. (The therapy will be discussed more fully in Chapters 8 and 9.)

Comparisons and competition induced by the perfection rule are usually intrafamilial as well as interfamilial. Within a family there will usually be at least one person winning the competition for rightness and at least one person losing it. It is an axiom for us in working with shame-bound families that if there is an obvious "good" person or an obvious "bad" person, the opposite polarity will be found in another person. To work with the problem requires working with the whole system of polarities, not just with the "bad" or symptomatic part.

This is a commonly occurring example of Bateson's (1972) concept of complementarity. The "good one" is usually good by taking the values of the family and fulfilling them in explicit and demonstrable ways, *in contrast* to someone else in the family who is "bad." Among children we commonly see at least one "good" one among a family of delinquents or one "bad" one among a family representing all of the stereotyped values in the culture. In a marriage this phenomenon can appear as the wife who is representing the proper social graces and trying to reform her alcoholic husband, who represents the "wild side," each polarity needing the other for definition.

The superficial therapeutic approach to human problems tries to get the "bad one," or the delinquent one, or the symptom bearer to improve or to feel better or to express more fully the positive side of the polarity. Such naive therapy focuses on the individual and the overt symptom, overlooking the dynamics of the complementary balance between the one who successfully does the "right" thing and the one who successfully highlights the "right" by providing negative contrast. It is as if there were one or more family members on the pedestal embodying what is "right" by the explicit values of the family and the culture, while one or more down beneath the pedestal loyally point to what is "right" by way of contrasting negative behavior. Each person, whether on the pedestal or beneath it, is incomplete and has a distorted human experience. Neither position leads to full development of personhood or authentic self-esteem. To effect fundamental change in the system will require change in the underlying perfectionism rule.

3) BLAME

If something doesn't happen as you planned, blame someone (yourself or someone else). Blaming is pervasive in the shame-bound family and in all relationships which have a strong shame component. The blame may be overt, as in the message, "If it weren't for you I would be happy." Often the blame is masked as something else. A woman thinks she is only expressing her feelings, but what she says is, "I feel that you always get upset when I'm doing my work and that stops me from accomplishing anything." In fact, she has expressed nothing at all about her own feelings. A personal question which asks "Why?" is usually an emotional trap for someone to blame themselves or justify why they are not blameworthy. "Why do you . . . ?" or "why don't you . . . ?" often pose as innocent questions but are loaded with bad feelings. Self-blame is a direct expression of the rule and can be highly controlling in relationships, in that it effectively grabs the initiative. While self-blame is painful, it keeps the blamer in charge of the interaction and thus reduces surprise.

In effect, a person's blaming behavior covers one's shame or projects it onto another person. When I focus on what you do to me, I feel a reduction in my own anxiety about myself. If, for example, I tell you that you never approach me warmly, I don't have to experience the vulnerable feeling of telling you how lonely or needy I feel. If I'm a shame-bound person, I cannot feel vulnerable or needy without being ashamed of it. So blaming becomes an automatic evasion of my deeper feelings.

In fact, any unexpected or unplanned occurrence can become a moment for blame, whether or not it is inherently negative. A flat tire while driving to work is understandably negative and in this system produces blame of oneself or someone else. But the delivery of a package by a parcel service three days before someone's birthday, instead of on the birthday, isn't inherently negative. Within this system it is liable to being perceived as ruining the sender's whole plan and someone is likely to be blamed.

The blame rule is activated to maintain the equilibrium of the system in those situations where the control rule breaks down. When security is sought through control as it is in this family system, even to the point of a compelling demand, the reality of life's unpredictability and uncontrollability invokes pervasive anxiety. Blame is the bitter salve habitually used by members of the system to regain the illusion of control. Whether the usual pattern is self-blame or blame of others, blaming always provides a reliable fall-back position of control and predictability when the first attempt to be in control or do things perfectly doesn't succeed. In this way, we see the interaction of the first three rules of control, perfection, and blame.

The first three rules are seen at work in the following example from a therapy session. The wife/mother was recounting how hard she tries to build relationships in her life and how "good" she is in her dealings with people, but she still ends up without a friend. The therapist responded empathically, warmly saying that the woman seemed "lonely." She was startled and then said, "I can't tolerate you putting me down like that. I'm not lonely! Why do you have to make my life harder than it already is?" For her to receive the empathy contained in the message would have been to allow some measure of interaction outside her control, i.e., she did not create or expect the empathy.

Her stylized response is loyal to the blame rule by falling back to blame when something surprising (such as a moment of personal warmth) begins to develop. In this negativism she has a reliable and consistent "friend" because she never has to exist in a time of uncertainty or vulnerability, wondering what will happen to her. As one person said, "Nothing ventured, nothing lost!" She can fall back on the blame response so instantly and habitually that she never has to become aware of even a momentary feeling of self-doubt or personal introspection.

Unfortunately, this woman and other members of her family who are loyal to these rules also miss the personal relationship development, the maturational process, which comes when we live through moments of anxiety or uncertainty in the interaction without immediately grasping for control and predictability. They miss learning about deeper relationships, which are spontaneous entities beyond the individual control of either person's ego.

4) DENIAL

Deny feelings, especially the negative and vulnerable ones like anxiety, fear, loneliness, grief, rejection, neediness, and caring. In its most extreme application, the denial rule produces a very cold system of relationships. People don't acknowledge genuine personal feelings even to themselves. In effect, the members of this system don't know they have the feelings at all. Development of our physical muscles and strength serves as an apt metaphor for development of emotional awareness and expression. In some families, physical strength and agility are enjoyed as a part of family life together through playing ball or doing labor. In other families, physical conditioning, strength, and athletic development are ignored and the capacities lay dormant. Likewise, comfort with feelings may either grow with experience in a family or be undeveloped. The experience of having deep and strong feelings is part of a relationship with oneself and part of the depth of relationship with others. It is learned with practice and increasing maturity when that is allowed into the family climate. A basic level of human feelings is present for all of us, but one's relationship to them will either be familiar and comfortable or denied, naive, and primitive.

There seem to be several ways in which a family style can accommodate this rule. In one family the interaction may be rigorously task-focused and practical, so that a person's feelings have no relevance or validity. This family gets its jobs done. Family members function well in less intimate relationships at work and school. Objective, outside measures of performance in our culture define them as successful. But they don't know each other as intimates. A personal relationship to one's own feelings and those of one's children or one's spouse has never developed in this family.

One such family we knew had a weekly Saturday night scenario in which one adolescent son would come home drunk and violent. He would threaten to beat everyone up and the father and another son would wrestle him to the floor and hold him down until he fell into his drunken sleep. On Sunday no one acknowledged the events of Saturday night, nor did they acknowledge that there was anything to acknowledge.

In another family the emphasis may be primarily upon the performance of roles. In this family, people see themselves and others as defined by their role as mother, father, sister, son. "This is how a father or mother is in a family." Role definition provides useful structure for family interaction in all families. But when the role becomes predominant, when it cannot be transcended by personal uniqueness, spontaneity and feelings, the family experience becomes form without substance, image without soul. When emphasis on role is combined with the perfectionism principle, people try to be the perfect parent or perfect son or daughter. What develops out of this dual emphasis is not just the superficiality of role dominated relationships, but a double-binding tyranny. "For me to be perfect in my role, I need you to play my complementary opposite. If I'm to be a perfect parent, I'm dependent upon my children being perfect to validate that I'm performing my role perfectly. It then follows that I'm most upset when their life experience or performance doesn't confirm that I'm doing it right." The sad product of this system is that each family member's sense of personhood lays undeveloped, and is fertile ground for shame.

5) UNRELIABILITY

Don't expect reliability and constancy in relationships. The roller coaster of mood swings has long been identified as a characteristic of the individual drug addict and alcoholic. This has been seen as the result of swings in body chemistry. The prototypical mood swing of the individual addict moves on the shame-bound cycle from personal tension and anxiety buildup in the control phase, to the "high" of the release phase, to the depression or regret of overt shame, which eventually leads back to the tension buildup. When a mood-altering chemical is involved, we can see that these mood changes occur in response to the physical effects of the chemical and quite regardless of the flow of events within a relationship. The changes may be experienced as puzzling or confusing by people in a relationship with a chemical user. Eventually the unpredictability will be incorporated into the expected pattern of the system and assumed that, "This is how relationships are." In looking at the many manifestations of shamebound families, we see that the whole system is involved with and incorporates these inconsistencies and unpredictable mood swings, regardless of the presence of mood-altering chemicals.

In the shame-bound system, with relationships remaining at an immature level, individuals are repeatedly disappearing on their emotional connections. Sometimes the disappearance is actively motivated by a deep sense of personal shame: "I'm not worthy or my behavior has made it too uncomfortable to stay in contact." In other instances the growth-inhibiting effect of the shame has created relationships in which individuals may have moments of nourishing rapport but have never learned an expectation of continuity.

We see in shame-bound families a prevalence of the cut-off relationships described by Murray Bowen (1978). These relationship cut-offs, in our view, are a product of the shame in the system and maintain the shame by freezing personal interactions at a point in time.

In the families we treat, mood swings, unpredictability, cut-offs and disappearances occur in some more or less subtle form in all members. They not only have accommodated to a member with unpredictable mood swings but have also taken "mood change" to be an acceptable reason for letting someone down. An example is the husband and wife who have a day in which they feel a great sense of rapport and connection. To be with then on that day one might think they had a fine relationship. However, within the system we are describing, that rapport can disappear unexpectedly and for no apparent reason. The husband might become tense and overly critical. The wife might become sullen and withdrawn for no obvious cause. Where an addiction is involved the switch is more closely tied in with the relationship to the substance than with anything that happened between the two people. In such an instance the person with the mood swing may have become preoccupied with his or her addictive behavior, bodily functions or phobias. Externally no change has occurred, but once again the experience of unreliability in the relationship is repeated. Where an addiction to a substance is not involved, people continue the pattern of unpredictable disappearances as a means to control the intimacy or to manipulate one another's responses.

Children growing up in this family will learn figuratively to toss their hat in the door before entering. They will not learn to expect a relationship to provide continuity or reliability of contact. This is a pattern that we have often seen maintained in the families of adult children of alcoholics and of other addicts, even though they have never had a problem with their own alcohol use.

We wish to emphasize at this point that the unreliability and inconsistency may look like a lack of caring or of emotional involvement. Indeed, this phenomenon is extremely destructive to relationships. But we think it is important for therapists to recognize this pattern when it exists and not mistake the coldness for lack of caring. When therapists help people terminate these relationships in divorce, as if they were leaving trouble behind, it provides unwitting support for the continuation of the pattern in the next relationship. Because there is no resolution, new learning never crystallizes. These patterns are much more amenable to change when they are confronted in the relationships where people have their attachments rather than in isolation after the split has taken place or in the subsequent marriage.

6) INCOMPLETENESS

Don't complete transactions. In the family with issues of shame it is common for disagreements to go unresolved for years. When a decision is called for within the relationship, the final conclusion somehow doesn't quite get drawn. It is easy for therapists, in their desire to respond to what clients describe as the problem, to miss the fact that yesterday's intense issue was never resolved. The issue may not be felt as a problem today but that's only because it was dropped, not because of resolution. People in this system often are unaware that they leave so much unresolved; when it is brought to their attention they may not know how to resolve or complete a transaction.

It is effective in this situation to use Virginia Satir's concept of the three parts of a completed transaction. In the first part a person *initiates* an interchange: "Let's go to the ball game." In the second part the other person *responds* to the first: "I would love to go if we can find a babysitter." In the third part the first person *responds to the response*: "Great! I'll check with our sitter and let you know what I come up with." The third part is the resolution. It may not actually come in the third exchange between two people but is the third phase in a completed transaction. In any discussion many exchanges occur before people reach the resolution phase and in the system we are describing it often doesn't happen at all. This third transaction is an acknowledgment that the response was received and gives something back in return. Resolution can take the form of getting clarity about a disagreement and an agreement to disagree. This, too, represents a resolution and is an aspect of rapport.

When the resolution doesn't occur, family members may be effectively avoiding a disagreement or they may be engaging endlessly in disagreements which lead nowhere. Super peaceful families, where members never disagree, may be puzzled by the symptoms they develop because they aren't aware of any strife in their relationships. What they don't know is that without open disagreement they lose the opportunity for resolution. Differences thus get hidden and perpetuated endlessly. Tension from hidden disagreements gets projected onto other members of the family or expressed in ways that seem mystifying. Tranquility may be strictly maintained in the marital relationship at the expense of symptoms developing in the child.

These placid families are difficult for family therapists to enter effectively. They are often treated cordially and pleasantly. Yet the peaceful surface is quite effective in preventing a therapist or anyone from getting to a more authentic understanding of what goes on in the relationships.

The chronically fighting family is similar, in that the relationship issues continue endlessly without resolution, and very often what appears on the surface to be the issue of the fight is only a distraction. So again, the therapist will have difficulty discerning what is authentic beneath this bellicose exterior.

The experience of persons in a system that emphasizes this rule is often confusion or puzzlement. They can become totally absorbed in discerning what is beneath this puzzling surface and in fact become enamored of making sense out of nonsense. On the contrary, other people in the system seem to so totally accept the messages of denial that they never look beneath the surface of any message. They take a message at its content level only and seem to be unusually naive or overly innocent in their understanding of human relationships. Whether a person wastes his or her energies trying to discern the meaning of nonsense or takes on a world view that blocks large parts of his/her experience, he/she is likely to be struggling with serious self-esteem issues because she/he is left with so much puzzlement or "mystification" (Laing, 1965).

7) NO TALK

Don't talk openly about disrespectful, shameful, abusive or compulsive behavior. This rule is so familiar to therapists working with families of chemical dependency, addiction, and abuse that it is commonly referred to as "the no-talk rule." It refers to the fact that the family system operates in such a manner that the reality of compulsive, harmful behavior never gets addressed directly. As such the system serves to protect and preserve the symptom, regardless of how fervently the individual family members yearn for it to cease. The rule also operates in sexual abuse families, where people suppress their suspicions about what is actually happening and never raise questions. Or they know what is happening and never tell anyone openly and clearly.

This rule is a hallmark of the kind of family we are speaking of, and it seems to be central to the preservation of the system. The "no-talk" rule may not always be hiding addictive or compulsive behavior. When family secrets exist, they form central pillars in the structure of a shame-bound system. We have often found instances of old secrets which one generation was not telling the next or one spouse was not telling the other. These foundation secrets always have an element of shame in them. Some examples of such secrets are suicide which was never acknowledged as a suicide or wasn't disclosed to the next generation, murder, extramarital affairs, prison terms in the past, illnesses that carried deep shame like tuberculosis or syphilis, and old incidents of abandonment or neglect in the family history.

It is important not to confuse this pathological "no-talk" rule with the more necessary privacy in which individuals and family units define their boundaries. In part, the identity of a family grows from common understandings and "secrets" that all family members understand are not to be disclosed to others. This kind of secret indeed serves to define who is inside and who is outside and provides a sense of security and respect in the relationships. The "no talk" rule is not based on choosing the option of privacy but on feelings of shame (whether they are conscious or not). Often there is a sense of no choice to disclose or hopelessness about disclosure.

8) DISQUALIFICATION

When disrespectful, shameful, abusive or compulsive behavior occurs, use disqualification and denial to reframe or disguise it. This rule serves to preserve the status quo of the system by avoiding the disruption in relationships which might be caused by the meaning of the behavior. It covers up the breach that occurs when values are violated. If the family value says that you shouldn't lose control of your anger when disciplining a child and that is exactly what has happened, the family system is preserved by messages that the child is very hard to teach or that "he stubbornly asked for more." In some families it becomes a family joke that the victim of abuse is a "rascal" who always needs more punishment. In other systems the problem may be overeating and gets reframed as "eating nourishing food." In the verbally abusive family the abuse is dismissed with a statement that "you have to understand her, she's really soft-hearted but doesn't know how to show it." In the sexually abusive family the abuse is disqualified as affection or the abuser gets laughed at as a "dirty old man."

Operation of this rule distorts one's perception of reality. Individual experience becomes partially defined out of existence by the system's process. What the person is left with are discrepancies between experience and the group's definition of that experience. This tends to leave people feeling deeply isolated, with grave doubts about their self-worth, and vulnerable to ever-widening divergence from cultural definitions of reality.

The eight rules of the shame-bound family, when used as an outline or prototype of the system, serve to alert us to the presence of the shame dynamic in underlying feelings and in the history of the family. Even when people are not identifying, "I need help with my shame," "I want help with my compulsive behavior," these rules will be apparent in their unique variation and will provide focus for the therapist's planning.

References

Bateson, G. (1972). *Steps to an ecology of mind.* New York: Ballantine Books.
Bowen, M. (1978). *Family therapy in clinical practice.* New York: Jason Aronson.
Farber, L. H. (1976). *Lying, despair, jealousy, envy, sex, suicide, drugs, and the good life.* New York: Harper & Row.
Ford, F. R., & Herrick, J. (1974). Family rules/ family life styles. *American Journal of Orthopsychiatry, 44,* 61–69.
Jackson, D. D. (1965). The study of the family. *Family Process, 4,* 1–20.
Laing, R. D. (1965). Mystification, confusion, and conflict. In I. Boszormenyi-Nagy & J. Framo (Eds.). *Intensive family therapy.* New York: Harper & Row.

6

THE INTERACTION OF
SHAME AND CONTROL

Samuel had an addictive relationship with exhibitionism. Since adolescence he episodically and secretly caught women by surprise and exposed himself to them. In his state of denial, Samuel had regarded each one of the hundreds of occurrences as an isolated loss of control. His pattern was to leave the house in the evening telling his wife and family that he was taking the dog for a walk or running to the market for some groceries. While he was out he would cruise favorite spots in search of a victim to expose himself to. After each event Samuel felt extremely shameful and self-hating and promised himself that he would never again engage in this behavior. Then he returned to his controlled and socially acceptable life. In effect he lived a double life, one of which was controlled and "on the record" and a secret life which was out of control and "off the record."

Samuel had become a clergyman in hopes that a religious life would provide the control he consciously willed. In retrospect the piety and intensified control in his life only seemed to make the secret release, when it came, that much more exciting and compelling. The shame and fear he felt after each episode further intensified his fervor in controlling all aspects of his experience. Overtly he threw himself into working harder, longer hours, demanding more of himself and his colleagues and being more critical of his wife and children. The phrase "monkey on his back" is an apt image for Samuel. The tortured tension he lived with was between the control that he consciously willed and the release from control which he found in the sexual excitement of exhibitionism.

This tension between control and release, with its potential for producing a mood-altering experience, is familiar to any adult. Anyone who has skied down a slope and felt the exhilaration of balancing speed, agility and grace with the difficulty and danger of the terrain knows the high it can produce. The sense of mastery and control a child feels walking along a narrow ledge or on a fence, knowing he or she could fall and yet does not, is another example. There can be a wonderful releasing rush of excitement in defying the injustice of someone in authority. When one masters the skill and discipline of a musical instrument or a dance so well that one can simultaneously follow the constraints of the form while letting oneself go, the tension between control and release provides a feeling of exhilaration or peace. These are examples in which shame is not a necessary element.

When shame or self-hate is introduced as an element in this equation, the picture changes to something more insidious. Small examples of the control-release tension with shame as an added element would be picking at a scab and continuing to do so after telling oneself to stop, or chewing one's fingernails until they hurt, or driving a car too fast for the conditions just for the thrill of speed.

When shame underlies the control and release it seems to intensify both sides of the tension. The oscillation between control and release is amplified. Shame makes the control dynamic more rigidly demanding and unforgiving and the release dynamic more self-destructive. The more intensely one controls, the more one requires the balance of release, and the more abusively or self-destructively one releases, the more intensely one requires control.

The diagram of the shame-bound cycle, introduced in Chapter 1, provides a graphic model for thinking about this repetitive process, so familiar to people who work with shame-bound families (see Figure 6).

This shame-bound cycle may be seen as a wheel represent-

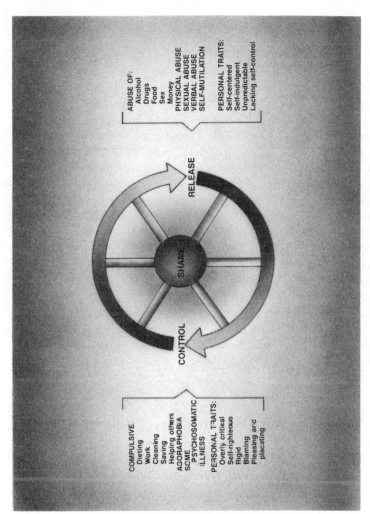

ABUSE OF:
Alcohol
Drugs
Food
Sex
Money
PHYSICAL ABUSE
SEXUAL ABUSE
VERBAL ABUSE
SELF-MUTILATION

PERSONAL TRAITS:
Self-centered
Self-indulgent
Unpredictable
Lacking self-control

RELEASE

SHAME

CONTROL

COMPULSIVE
Dieting
Work
Cleaning
Saving
Helping others
AGORAPHOBIA
SOME
PSYCHOSOMATIC
ILLNESS

PERSONAL TRAITS:
Overly critical
Self-righteous
Rigid
Blaming
Pleasing and
placating

Figure 6 The shame-bound cycle

ing the movement of one individual from control to release
to control to release, etc., with shame as the hub. Shame is
experienced differently by the person at different points on
the cycle. After the release one might feel an overt sense of
shame, as in the morning-after remorse following an alcoholic
binge. With the control phase one's shame is likely to be more
covert, covered by self-righteousness or irritability.

This cycle is not a moderate process. In the control phase
a person will display excesses of control, both in attempts to
control oneself and in efforts to control the responses of others.
The release phase is not simply relaxation or loosening of control. It is a breakout, an escape from the pressures of control
and shame. Thus, an intense oscillation develops. It is a runaway reactive process with little grounding in a sense of personhood. The more the individual attempts to control, the
more demanding is the need for release. The more one escapes
into the release phase, the more uncontrolled one will feel and
thus the more one will attempt to compensate with more control. Releases are at different frequencies for different people. Some will control for long intervals of months or even
years between releases, while others will find several releases
in a day. Regardless of the frequency, the interplay of control and release is significant.

In a normal family, limits serve useful functions and controls provide predictability and safety, along with some frustration. They make it possible for children and adults to feel
a measure of security and power in a fundamentally insecure
world. But in shame-bound families, limits and controls are
often applied as a single answer to all anxiety or emotional
pain. "Do it better!" "Anticipate the problems!" "Be an achiever!"
There is little of the wisdom that the movement and process
of life also have benevolent forces. Individuals in these families seldom say, "Things have a way of working out!" Limits
and controls as the single answer become stifling, suffocat-
ing, even deadly.

Bateson (1972, p. 311) observed this oscillation in his work
with alcoholics and matched "the sobriety (control phase) and
the intoxication (release phase), such that the latter may be

seen as an appropriate subjective correction for the former."
He observes:

> The friends and relatives of the alcoholic commonly
> urge him to be "strong," and to "resist temptation."
> . . . the alcoholic himself – while sober (in the control
> phase) – commonly agrees with their view of his "prob-
> lem." He believes that he could be, or, at least, ought
> to be "captain of his soul." But it is a cliché of alco-
> holism that after "that first drink," the motivation to
> stop drinking is zero (release phase). Typically the
> whole matter is phrased overtly as a battle between
> "self" and "John Barleycorn." Covertly the alcoholic
> may be planning or even secretly laying in supplies
> for the next binge, but it is almost impossible (in the
> hospital setting) to get the sober alcoholic to plan his
> next binge in an overt manner. He cannot, seeming-
> ly, be the "captain" of his soul and overtly will or com-
> mand his own drunkenness. The "captain" can only
> command sobriety – and then not be obeyed. (Bateson,
> 1972, p. 312)

Bateson asserts that "the alcoholic" is caught up in an
"unusually disastrous variant of the Cartesian dualism, the
division between Mind and Matter, or, in this case, between
conscious will, or 'self' and the remainder of the personality"
(Bateson, 1972, p. 313).

We have generalized this creative insight about alcoholism
to the many problems where control and release seem to be
at war. The "unusually disastrous" nature of this dualism
which Bateson identified in alcoholism (and which we now
find in all the other addictions and compulsions so commonly seen in psychotherapists' offices) is explained by the element of shame. While we all live in a culture shaped by the
epistemological split between mind and matter, the greater
one's sense of shame, the more uncontrolled and destructive
the effect of this split appears to be.

Bateson says that the 12-step program of Alcoholics Anonymous (AA) is so successful with alcoholism because it confronts the dualism in the first two steps. AA calls for its members to "surrender" this willful, controlling outlook in the first step and in the second step to accept that a greater power can restore sanity. He admires this approach and reframes it philosophically as a change to a "more correct epistemology," one more consistent with our advances in cybernetics and systems theory. When we observe several of the subsequent steps of the AA program, it is clear that they deal with issues of shame and guilt, accountability, repair of relationships, and reliability, all of which are crucial to the shame-bound cycle. This gives a better theoretical understanding of why the Alcoholics Anonymous program has been so successful.

RELEASE PHASE

The release phase, whether it represents compulsive drinking or any of the other releases and escapes, is a personal experience of "losing" oneself. It is an escape from the oppressive rules of the system while remaining loyal to them. In the violation or loss of control the individual feels a relaxation of his or her conscious will. At the same time the reliability of the method of escape is paradoxically consistent with the rule demanding control, i.e., since a drug or a ritualized behavior provides a reliable release, this reliability also gives a sense of power and control even in the release.

While experiencing the relief of escape, a person may also experience the terror of loss of control — or the violation of fundamental self-respect and care. This internally motivated abuse of self can be as shaming as any boundary invasion or abusive, demeaning behavior from an external source. When one has been demeaned one feels demeaned. An assault upon oneself is shaming whether one is the victim of another person's attack or of one's own violation of self as in self-mutilation or compulsive drunkenness. In some cases the release takes the form of a binge, in other cases the release is what we call "controlled use" and represents a more routinized controlled mood change. Whether the release behavior takes the form of compulsive shopping, eating, sex, drinking, raging, or whatever, it is followed by a more or less overt feeling of shame. At this time the person is feeling, most acutely, the effects of a violation of self. There are many variations and exceptions in which the subjective feeling of shame is not overt following the release. A person may be ashamed of feeling ashamed and in effect hide from the truth of even this message coming from the remnant of a self. In this instance he is already fleeing into rationalization and justifications to cover the shame.

The release phase generally is shrouded in secrecy, denial and disqualification, as described under the "no talk" rule and disqualification rule in Chapter 5. It is not rare for both the individuals involved in the release activity and the members of their family to sincerely not know or acknowledge that they have a compulsive, abusive pattern. Sometimes it is a secret. The release is often not simply secret but subtle, vague, or obscure, and identification of specific compulsive release behaviors is difficult. Therapists must be self-aware in looking for such behaviors. We have seen people, in their zeal for uncovering hidden or secret behavior, take on the appearance of zealots on a witch hunt. A therapist must be worldly wise about the fact that what is first seen is often the tip of the iceberg, and be prepared to see more or to actively look for more below the surface. This worldly wisdom, however, is to be distinguished from a therapist's personal commitment to "save" someone by searching out and uncovering hidden addictions and abuses. Until some relationship of trust exists, racing into deeper levels of disclosure and honesty than clients are ready for can be invasive and abusive in itself.

CONTROL PHASE

An individual in the control phase is trying to get control over her or his life, or some aspect of it. This can take many forms such as, work, cleaning, moralism and judging of others, self-improvement campaigns, harsh dieting, or miserliness.

Persons in this phase are commonly called "hard to live with" because of the intensity of their approach to life and the fact that they may be very critical of those around them or intrusive by their demands and directives, manipulations or helpfulness.

Whereas the release phase may be destructive to relationships by its unreliability and abandonment effect, the control phase can be equally destructive to relationships by the failure to let people be or to allow the relationship to flow in a natural process. A person in this phase lacks true self-awareness and will generally explain relationship difficulties by blaming others. After all, aren't they clearly trying hard to do everything right?

We hear from adults who were reared by an alcoholic parent how critical and demanding that parent was. The child seldom received a message from the parent that he or she was accepted for who he/she was, without reservation. The parent's self-hate, intensity and anxiety got passed on to the child through endless demands and criticisms.

In a case of psychosomatic problems we worked with a woman who would obsess about her physical processes. If she walked up a flight of stairs fast enough to elevate her heart rate slightly, she would begin to worry that it would not naturally slow down and would lead to a heart attack. The more anxious she became about her heart, the less likely it was to slow down and she would then call her doctors or go to a hospital emergency room to get control of her heart rate. She was so shameful and so lacking in trust in her own physical process that she could not believe that her body would work like other people. The "magic" words by a physician, "You are OK," brought immediate relief.

A therapist who works with advanced cases of alcoholism commented that he would have expected the skid row alcoholic to have lost all attempts to keep some order in his life. Contrary to his expectation, when he visits these victims in their own rooms, he may find them scrubbing the floor or meticulously arranging their possessions on a shelf as a way of maintaining a specific area of control.

While all individuals in a shame-bound system relate to this cycle, not everyone actively moves around it. Some people in the system primarily represent the control aspect of the cycle and are balanced by someone else who provides the release. We find them to be overinvolved or fused in that relationship, although they may not consciously value the other person's behavior. Our culture tends to view the representative of control protectively, as a long-suffering saint. The spouse of the alcoholic, for instance, is regarded by neighbors or friends with admiration and pity for her or his long-suffering endurance. People in this position are as loyal and as trapped by the system as those representing the release phase. They're called codependent because, although they may not have a direct dependency on a release behavior, they have a close relationship with someone else who provides a vicarious release.

In families with highly developed shame dynamics one will find multiple symptoms of both control and release. Children growing up in a family with an alcoholic or otherwise compulsive/abusive parent, integrate this cycle as part of their own system with shame at the center. They have not had a model or intimate support for the development of a sense of personhood. As adults, when they establish families of their own, some version of the cycle continues, often disguised as something different. Perhaps the addiction of one generation gets replaced unwittingly by another addiction or other symptoms in the next. We knew a family in which both parents had come from poor, deprived, and painful childhoods. The mother's family was abandoned by an alcoholic father when she was eight years old. Her mother raised the children under difficult circumstances with a moral, self-righteous fervor. They had survived using this attitude but it perpetuated the shame-bound cycle. They never dealt with their own part in the cycle and thus perpetuated it. They simply thought they were better off without the "trouble-maker" father.

When this family appeared for therapy, the 14-year-old daughter (now the third generation we know of) was experiencing many signs of anxiety on the control side of the cycle, in the form of obsessiveness about her grades and homework, sleeplessness, and irritability.

Many symptoms of the shame-bound family are manifestations of the overdeveloped control phase. Anorexia nervosa, as a deadly overcontrol of eating, could be seen in this light. The starving client's focus on feeding other people, which is so often a part of the syndrome, represents a vicarious release. Agoraphobia is a very practical control over one's life, and there may be a certain amount of security in knowing that one's fears will protect one from a loss of control. We worked with an agoraphobic client who would get increasingly anxious as he got further from home. His case history revealed that before he developed a phobia, he traveled extensively for a government agency, but was painfully obsessed and frenzied with out-of-control sexual behavior while out of town. Clearly, his agoraphobia served a control function for his compulsive sexual behavior which, though still present, was now experienced far less frequently. Other examples of compulsivity in the control phase are saving or hoarding money to an extreme (having several secret bank accounts, unknown even to one's spouse), religiosity (the practice of a religion so rigidly, perfectionistically, and focused on rules that it stifles life rather than enriching it), workaholism (the obsessive, compulsive use of a career or busy-ness with tasks to avoid the flow of relationships and feelings), and the child-centered couple who find all their meaning vicariously through the lives of their children.

While there is extensive shame underlying the control phase, it generally is not overt, as in the release phase. This phase of the cycle elicits the other side of the shame coin, i.e., denial and self-righteousness. People who have managed to gain control of themselves and/or others are likely to feel that they have avoided the gutter and, by their own force of will, achieved a superior status. People who are caught on this cycle rarely have a genuine peer relationship because they cannot submit to the lack of control. They feel either superior or inferior to all peers or are so actively attempting to please and be "nice" that they cannot relax into a relationship of equality.

SHAME-CONTROL MODEL OF ABUSIVE FAMILY INTERACTION

The grid in Figure 7 was developed as a way of talking with abusive families about their own process. It is common to be sitting in a therapy room with a family and hear about abusive behavior which has occurred in the recent past. As they talk with the therapist there may be no overt evidence of the abusive behavior. They sincerely deny that it will happen again. They can be quite convincing to any outsider because

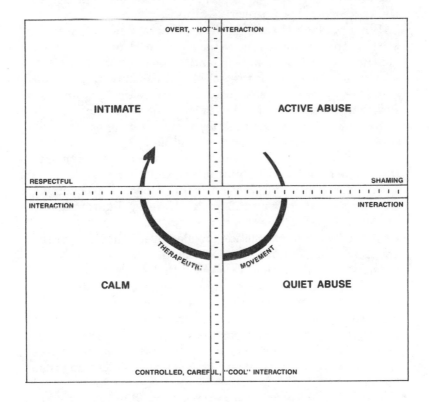

Figure 7 Shame-control model of abusive family interaction

they believe that the most recent excursion into active abuse will be the final one. What the family often believes is that the loss of control is the problem, or the anger is the problem, or taking the first drink is the problem. What they do not see is that the constant in their process is their shame and the shaming interaction. They try to remain in control but their tighter control does not allow for much engagement between people. Control as the single answer does not work if the system is to continue as a vital organism. With little possibility to invent more respectful release and engagement, they will inevitably break out again, perhaps with one person as the representative, into active abuse.

When we look at their family interaction as outsiders we see that they do indeed move back and forth on an intensity continuum — between "hotter" and "cooler" interaction. But, they do not move on the respect-shame continuum. In the active abuse phase someone may be overtly abusing another family member or himself and in the controlled phase people may be staring daggers, making demeaning comments, failing to accept each other's reality, sulking, or giving someone the silent treatment. The family process remains shaming to its members but varies in intensity and overtness.

A continuum of interaction from respectful to shaming was introduced in Chapter 2 (p. 21). Here we diagram family process by intersecting this horizontal continuum with a vertical continuum of interaction labelled overt, "hot" at one end and controlled, careful, "cool" at the other.

On the respectful side of this hypothetical grid, interaction includes expressing one's thoughts and feelings, listening to each other, and acknowledging the interchange. Respect means engagement with one another as separate persons. Shaming interaction is the direct opposite. It is failure to acknowledge another person. It includes presumptions about someone's thoughts or feelings, boundary invasions and demeaning communication.

The *active abuse quadrant* represents individual behavior or family interaction in which some kind of overt abuse is occurring. It is tangible. It is the kind of behavior that may be against the law, or is physically or emotionally excessive and harmful to oneself or someone else. All of the release behaviors of the shame-bound cycle fall within this quadrant.

Behaviors in the *quiet abuse quadrant* may have as devastating an impact on the human spirit as active abuse. They are less obvious in their undermining and assaultiveness, so that people are less likely to know why they feel bad or what the stress in their family is about. It is in this quadrant where the threats to abandon come, where the blaming and silent treatment is used. While the behavior is not actively abusive it is continuous with and integral to active abuse. This is the quadrant where most abusive families spend most of their time. The active abuse behavior may involve a small fraction of the family's total time; the rest of the time is spent in controlled tension of quietly abusive interchanges. One of the features of this distant, "cool" behavior is that it seems to generate potential for more intense contact which breaks out as abuse. Some families exist in this quadrant and never break out into active abuse. In these families the potential for explosion isn't relieved by a break-out, and tension exists which is felt by the most vulnerable member(s) as hypersensitivity to anger, fear of criticism, or of retaliation. The control behaviors of the shame-bound cycle fall within either this quadrant or the calm quadrant.

The *calm quadrant* represents behavior which is decent, orderly, and may be rather careful or conscious of form. People are nice to each other here, they listen respectfully, they do not intrude upon one another. When family interaction stays for too long in this quadrant it becomes stagnant, boring and dead. Everyone needs to have some novelty, some unpredictability and spontaneous contact in their relationships. This quadrant represents an important aspect of vital family process but it isn't a goal to achieve and stop at.

We often see families with alcoholism or physical abuse in their history getting stuck in this quadrant. Many have had successful therapy for the abuses in their past; others have moved into another life stage or matured out of the abusiveness. For others the abuse was in the prior generation. The symptoms they develop are the quieter ones listed on the control side of the shame-bound cycle. If they do find release it is into the less hostile, less assaultive behaviors on the release side.

This quadrant can be the place where families get stuck, thinking that since they have escaped the shaming and disrespectful life in their history their growth is complete. It is impressive how frightening loss of control remains for them. Their old internal association of loss of control with pain and abuse continues. They have not learned to accept and integrate the "darker side" of their selves. They have few models for respectful, spontaneous contact. Prior experience has shown them that when controls are dropped and people become less deliberate and less conscious, someone gets hurt, abused or shamed. So they cling to the respectful, controlled distance in their relationships.

Time in this quadrant is a necessary phase in a family's recovery process. But, after months or years, if they haven't found respectful ways of being more spontaneous, they begin to wonder if their marriage is empty. Their relationships — or life as a whole — may seem dead and they need additional help in learning how to play and have conflict and engage with each other in respectful spontaneity. They are still caught on the shame-bound cycle and need to learn that they still have powerful feelings, like self-hate and fear, which they can accept within themselves without compulsion to abuse.

Other people come to therapy having developed fears, feelings of personal emptiness and even phobias after a period of time in this phase. They have had the opportunity to begin a relationship with themselves, and in the process have experienced strong feelings and new awarenesses that are unfamiliar and frightening. They need the reassurance of a road map. A therapist can be a coach to them with their new feelings, helping them learn to accept them as a normal part of the development of personhood.

The *intimate, spontaneous quadrant* includes family interaction which is close and nurturant, playful, confrontive and conflictual. There is much contact between people in this quadrant, and an underlying premise that everyone is respected.

Families that are free to move into this quadrant have much more flexibility than abusive families. They have a flow which is less self-conscious or contrived. Family members can lose themselves in this interaction, letting go in safe and respectful relationships. This is not an idealistic trouble-free family experience. No one expects perfection. Mistakes are made, people get hurt and angry, boundaries get violated, and everyone is accountable for behavior. There is always a way back. Repair is expected and available and is brought into the dialogue of relationships. Even the experience of shame is possible and is brought into the relationship dialogue rather than walled off as a secret or distorted and used destructively.

Three interactional behaviors – touch, humor, and the use of nicknames – will illustrate the different quality of interaction in each quadrant on this grid. Touch in the active abuse quadrant is invasive, hurtful (either physically or emotionally), and done in an exploitive or using manner. Here we see people getting beaten, children getting forced to have their fingers burned, coerced sexual contact, and all of the other blatant abuses by touch. The touch may be seductive, hostile, or loaded with dominance-submission messages.

In the quiet abuse quadrant touch is more controlled and careful, tighter, still abusive but less obviously so. A harsh and hurtful grip on a child's or spouse's arm and too rough play that inflicts injury are examples of quietly shaming touch. Or it may be mutual agreement between consenting adults to use one another. Although the messages are less obvious than in active abuse, they are just as invasive, manipulative, hostile or filled with dominance-submission issues.

Touch in the calm quadrant is careful, controlled and respectful. It might be in the form of a handshake, a hug, a goodbye kiss, or sexual contact, but it will not be spontaneous, risky or surprising in any way. It is completely predictable, sometimes ritualized, even perfunctory, and may, in the extreme, seem hollow. It is generally nonthreatening and it takes place under a general understanding of permission or propriety.

In the intimate quadrant touch is active, easy to understand, and well meaning. It may be nurturing, as in a caress or embrace, or it may be firm and directive, as when a person bodily points someone in a direction. It may also be surprising or powerful or spontaneous within the bounds of respect and permission.

Humor in the active abuse quadrant is laughter at someone's expense. Sarcasm is prevalent. It is hostile, poisonous humor and provides a way for people to get together by laughing at someone in a demeaning or disqualifying way.

In the subtle abuse quadrant humor is less obvious in its demeaning message. The victim of the humor is left feeling bad but not sure why, or wondering if there is something wrong with the way he or she interpreted it.

Little humor is to be found in the calm quadrant and probably what is there is more impersonal, not carrying hurtful messages. In the intimate quadrant people may well laugh at one another's foibles and make jokes of one another's weaknesses or uniqueness but this comes out of intimate knowing and basic understanding and respect. It is humor about humanness and rearranges the familiar in surprising ways.

Nicknames on the shame side of the grid are of the name-calling, put-down variety. They are more obvious on the hot end of the continuum and more subtle on the cool end. These names are cutting and demeaning, like "stupid," "fatso," "fag," and racial slurs.

On the respectful side of the grid, "pet" names are shared. Such names as "Stinkie," "Poopsie," and "Gorilla" might be used in this way. The names may, in fact, be diminutive or humorous but their use expresses a special knowing and a closeness to the person. They define an endearing, respectful relationship. When the very same pet name is used by someone outside the close relationship it might be considered a disrespectful intrusion.

Any family may find itself occasionally interacting in any one of the quadrants we have described. In fact, it is unlikely that many families could not recognize themselves in behavioral scenarios that fit each type. There is a paradox in the fact that families that often find themselves interacting in the intimate spontaneous category probably range more widely in their behavior on this grid than other families. By definition, intimate respectful interaction includes the flexibility of a lapse into disrespect, followed by authentic repair. A family that is in serious psychological difficulty is less fluid in its movement on this grid. Interaction among family members is more stereotyped. They are stuck, predominantly interacting in one or two of the three quadrants dominated by shame and/or control.

Therapeutic movement begins with the stopping of the active abuse. Sometimes the limit is set on abusive behavior by therapeutic contract, sometimes the court has ordered protection for a victim, and sometimes a person must be hospitalized for his/her own protection.

When the active abuse stops a family is predominantly in the quiet abuse category. Although the behavior is limited, the underlying shame is not so easily identified or changed. This will not be unfamiliar to their system since the family members have had experiences in this quadrant before. Now the therapist and clients begin to uncover the implicit shame and denial and to teach and learn more respectful behaviors.

As family members recognize the shame and learn respectful, enhancing interaction, they move into the calm quadrant. At this point family behavior takes on the surface form of respect – this may be a brand-new experience for them. They are now in the position of having given up the protection of familiar, abusive escapes and having a format or a recipe for how to become whole persons. It is a necessary climate which supports and makes growth possible within a safer context. They can be overtly respectful now. They have learned the talk of feelings and therapy. Yet, it is still a controlled, careful system.

Movement into the spontaneity of the intimate quadrant is very frightening for a family with a history of abuse. While release has provided a way to have contact in the past, it has always been paired with shame, abuse, and chaos. Carl Whitaker (private communication) has said that the experience of abuse in a family is similar to having poison ivy. Once you have had it you are hypersensitive or allergic to it for the rest of your life. It takes courage and faith on the part of both the clients and the therapist and some active coaching to help people move beyond the recipes for mental health into authentic, intimate, and generative personal relationships.

Reference

Bateson, G. (1972). *Steps to an ecology of mind.* New York: Ballantine Books.

7

ADDICTIONS: RESERVOIRS OF FAMILY SHAME

There is no crisis without a gift for you in its hands. We seek those crises because we need their gifts. (Bach, 1977)

One of the most clearly identifiable aspects of shame in families is addictive behavior. The addiction becomes a central organizing principle for the system, maintaining the system as well as its shame. When we address addiction in a family, we open the door to the family's shame. When families face their addiction crises, they meet opportunities for fundamental growth and change in the system. When families break the rules by stopping compulsive behaviors, they find the potential of the gift of intimacy, but also their great, overwhelming fear of intimacy.

The word "addiction" is used lightly and accepted colloquially in our culture. It is not unusual for someone to say, "I'm addicted to ice cream (or books or racquetball)," when he or she means "I really like ice cream alot." According to *Webster's* the root word "addicere" means "to give oneself up" or "to devote or surrender (oneself) to something habitually or obsessively."

While compulsivity is an integral aspect of shame, not all compulsive behaviors are addiction. When a person forms a primary relationship with a substance or an activity, we call the behavior addictive. At some point what is called a habit or repetitive behavior can be called an addiction. Clinically, it is often difficult to determine just when a habit becomes an addiction. Our criterion is: "When you can't control when you start or stop the activity, when it begins to damage you and your close relationships, you're addicted" (Milkman & Sunderwirth, 1984, p. 12).

Milkman and Sunderwirth (1984) state that compulsiveness, loss of control, and continuation of harmful behavior are not merely temporary reactions to stress but instead constitute a predictable progression through definite stages. In recent years we have seen the development of specific programs for various addictions identifiable at specific stages. While many families have successfully completed treatment programs for chemical dependency or anorexia nervosa or bulimia, these control-oriented, shame-bound systems retain their addictive dynamics. Families at the high end on the continuum of shame often manifest multiple addictions. It is not uncommon to see compulsive drug use accompanied by compulsive overeating or starving or work habits in one or more family members.

One of the most important adjuncts to our therapy with addiction is the use of 12-step groups. These mutual help groups meet regularly and focus on a single problem such as alcoholism, bulimia, narcotics, overeating, etc., with one stipulation for membership—the desire to abstain from the compulsive behavior. AA is the most widely known and the original 12-step group. Others are Narcotics Anonymous, Overeaters Anonymous, Gamblers Anonymous and Sex Addicts Anonymous. For family members and friends of addicts, similar 12-step groups meet to focus on their powerlessness to control the behavior of the addicted partner. Examples are: Al-Anon (for those in relationships with alcoholics), Al-Ateen (for children of alcoholics), O-Anon (those in relationships with compulsive overeaters), Gamanon (those in relationships with compulsive gamblers), Co-SAA, (co-sex addicts) etc.

Participants share their experiences openly and honestly with one another and learn from one another. This is the opposite experience of the secretive, shame-bound compulsivity and defensiveness. Clients face their powerlessness, receive support from the group and gain acceptance. This mutual vulnerability and "letting go" provides a way for a person to transcend the control paradox. It results in what the 12-step program calls a spiritual recovery – a recovery in which the human spirit (which had been flattened during compulsive behaviors) begins to unfold, making it possible for the client to connect on an emotional and human level with other group members. The 12 steps refer to 12 statements or directions for recovery beginning with the powerlessness of the individual's control attempts, personal inventories of guilt and shame, repair of wrongs, and moving to step 12, where the focus is on reaching out to other addicts.

We have learned that the treatment of one addictive behavior does not automatically eradicate compulsivity from the system. Treating addiction is similar to trying to catch a fish in the water with your bare hands. Just when you think you have a good hold on it, it darts away in another direction and the chase begins anew. The following case illustrates the elusiveness of addiction.

Ed and Jane and their children were in therapy following treatment for Ed's alcoholism. In AA, Ed had found his day-to-day acknowledgment of turning to his "higher power" brought him some peace in his abstinence from alcohol and a place to report honestly on his feelings. Jane received support from her Al-Anon group, where she was learning to stop controlling Ed and work only on herself. Their children attended Al-Ateen and had a safe place to talk about their feelings.

The family worked well in therapy and had made considerable progress, yet an invisible dragon loomed large in the room for, at times, the work would seemingly fall into a hole. After these sessions, we wondered aloud about the therapy, but told each other that the family *was* making progress and that perhaps the problem was just our wanting more closeness for them than they wanted for themselves.

Then one day came the eruption. Ed arrived a few minutes early for a family therapy appointment, barged into the ther-

apy room, and paced back and forth, exclaiming, "Look, I've
had it! Eight years of AA and Jane in Al-Anon and the kids
in their self-help groups, and I'm still hooked! . . . I can't stay
away from the women in Chicago!" The dragon was out:
Throughout his marriage Ed had led a secret sex life shrouded
in deep shame and pain. Now we could begin to pursue the
compulsive behavior again, this time the apparent sexual
addiction.

At one point Ed said in aggravation, "My God, just what
group do I belong to? I could go to one for alcoholism, another for overeating, and now a group for sexual addiction!"
In his anger he realized that he needed to examine his history of compulsive sexual contact with women. While a treatment program had helped him quit drinking, it had had no
effect on the underlying addiction. We saw the need to explore in depth the range of compulsive behaviors in the family
and to work with the controlling behaviors surrounding the
compulsivity. Obviously, the successful work that this family
had already done had prepared its members for the next stage
of their growth, i.e., family therapy to face their shame and
related compulsivity.

Addiction is a manifestation of the system, and becomes
a supporting pillar in the system; it is much more than one
single, identifiable "disease." Yet, addiction presents itself as
a primary, identifiable pattern in an individual. While the individual "disease" must be treated, the compulsivity in the
system does not vanish with one person's individual treatment; the family is a part of the addiction and must be a part
of the treatment.

Various patterns of addiction are recognizable by specific
characteristics and presenting symptoms. In order for therapists to work with the broad base of family dynamics maintaining the shame, they must identify or uncover the central,
organizing principles of the system in the form of specific addictions in individuals. Sometimes this means sending individual family members to treatment programs in which the
whole family will be involved. After the addictive *behavior*

has ceased, the family is more emotionally available to one another as well as to the therapist.

CHEMICAL ADDICTIONS

The most commonly recognized addiction in our culture is chemical dependency. Since 1957, when the American Medical Association declared alcoholism to be a disease, we have seen great progress in the treatment of alcoholism. Perhaps the greatest growth has occurred in programs where the whole family, not just the alcoholic or drug dependent person, were treated. In elucidating the dynamics of substance-abusing families, Stanton and Todd (1982) have clearly shown how substance abuse is functional in the family system, and is strongly woven into the family's interpersonal world (Elkin, 1984). Stanton (1985) states that hard-core drug addicts hold the lowest status among chemical addictions, deepening their families' struggles with shame.

The addicted family is not always clearly identifiable clinically. In Chapter 3 we discussed the masks of shame; they are also the masks of addiction. The therapist should look for specific cues. The addicted family can present itself anywhere on the continuum of drug dependence. Polarization of feelings — from intense affect to no affective expression whatsoever — is common. Bowen (1978, p. 267) has stated that family members who are most dependent on the drinking person are often more overtly anxious than the one who drinks. The more the family members are threatened, the more anxious they get, the more they become critical, the greater the emotional isolation of the alcoholic.

Family members, whether present at the session or not, are typically overly involved with the drug abuser. They become increasingly "self-conscious, preoccupied with love/hate feelings about the alcoholic/drug abuser and about themselves . . . and they may experience physical, psychological, social and characterological impoverishment as well. The family becomes an emotional survival system, trying to cure the problem, and/or to ignore it, and/or to live with it — involved in a rigid stereotyped pattern of maladaptive behavior that simply maintains the problem" (Williams, 1984).

Despite their preoccupation with the user, family members may not talk about his or her chemical abuse. Often, the drug use may seem peripheral or minimal. It falls to the therapist to probe and decipher the code and give it the significance it deserves.

Therapists can probe for chemical addictions by looking at the family history and genogram on intake. Also, they can openly ask about all drug use, prescription and other. Skin discolorations, physical symptoms involving the liver, relationship struggles, and emotional shutdowns, depression, and emotional family cut-offs can all point to chemical addiction. Exaggerated sex-role behavior, i.e., the macho man or the helpless woman, is also a clue. Often, when we suspect chemical abuse, we ask clients not to use any chemicals while they are in therapy. Their response is often a clue to possible abuse. Often parents enter into therapy to "do something" about their adolescent's drug abuse, thereby protecting their alcoholic marriage.

When people hear the word "drugs," they typically think of "hard" drugs—heroin and cocaine. However, ten times as many people are dependent on prescription drugs as are dependent on heroin. Many people do not consider alcohol a drug. When we speak of chemical addictions, we refer to all drugs, including alcohol. While there are many chemical addictions, we find the following classification helpful.

Stimulants

Amphetamines (including most diet pills, cocaine, and speed) affect the body's arousal systems by increasing the level of electrical activity in the brain and producing a "rush." Consequently, stimulants are often used to heighten sexual pleasure.

Sex researchers are actively studying the strong relationship between sexual concerns and drug use; some find that almost 50 percent of those seeking sex therapy suffered from drug abuse—their own or their partner's (Coleman, 1982).

Depressants

Depressants (including alcohol) decrease the electrical activity of the cortical arousal system and slow bodily functions and awareness. They also affect the electrical activity of the limbic system (the portion of the brain controlling emotional responses.)

Like stimulants, depressants are directly linked to sexual concerns. Alcohol use can cause secondary impotence in men and anorgasmia in women. Because a rebalancing of the blood androgen level occurs after cessation of alcohol abuse, many men in alcoholism recovery have difficulty achieving or maintaining an erection. The problem, though temporary, forces many men to find alternative expressions of affection and is confounded because the alcohol enabled them to avoid intimacy.

Alcohol can also act as a behavioral stimulant by lowering inhibitions. Its use grants many people the permission they want to be more open and adventurous sexually. Many people maintain their cycle of shame by acting out sexually and then numbing the shame with alcohol, only to repeat the cycle again.

Hallucinogens

Marijuana, hashish and LSD act directly on the brain. Controversy concerning the effects of these drugs abounds. However, the placebo effect is acknowledged and at the time of this writing, both sides of the issue concerning hallucinogens' harmful effects are equally well supported by research data.

Nicotine

This addiction takes its toll: 350,000 smoking-related deaths and a $13 billion medical bill annually are figures reported by Goodman (Boston Globe, March 29, 1985). Until recently cigarette smoking has been one of the most popular and accepted forms of addictive behaviors, often shown with alcohol in ads. Despite public service messages about the harmful effects of cigarette smoking and the warnings printed on cigarette packages, little or no mention is made of the danger of addiction. With increased attention to smoking's harmful side effects, the public can no longer be unaware. Only addiction can account for the continuance of a behavior that contributes to lung cancer, lip cancer caused by pipes, as well as damage to other organs caused by nicotine and tars.

Smoking can be related to issues of intimacy. Smokers can smoke alone; cigarettes are readily available and provide a means to avoid closeness with others. Many people start smoking to relieve anxiety, but soon experience increased anxiety after smoking several cigarettes, a cigar or pipeful. A cigarette can provide instant intimacy, with the smoker in full charge of the "taking in." What the smoker does not realize at that moment is that the cigarette may be betraying him or herself. Often we have seen victims of sexual abuse smoking over two packages of cigarettes a day; when they quit smoking, clients have found many buried feelings.

Family members talk about the shame they experience when they cannot quit or find themselves "sneaking out" for a cigarette after they have announced they have quit smoking. They feel badly that they have broken their promises to themselves and others and feel shameful about their feelings of failure. Many parents often state their regret about the modeling they give their children.

Another clinical issue we see is control — family members attempting to control the smoking of a family member or setting limits for smoking in specific areas of the home. Some people have used smoking as a metaphor for their relationship, i.e., "I'd be more attracted to you if you didn't smell up everything with smoke." While cigarette smoking does not wreak the same havoc as alcohol and other drugs, nicotine is a harmful drug and its use can adversely affect relationships.

Caffeine

Many people enjoy their habit of drinking coffee, tea, or cola drinks containing caffeine. For others, it has become an addiction. Indeed, when Dr. John Minton (1984) of Ohio State

University asked 47 patients to make a hypothetical choice between eliminating caffeine from their diets or undergoing surgery for a caffeine-related medical problem, 27 chose surgery.

Pharmacologists consider more than 250 mg. of caffeine (two to three cups of coffee per day) to be the critical line between safe and excessive use. Ten percent of the U.S. population consumes more than 10 cups of coffee a day, or about 1 gm. of caffeine. This is four times the amount considered hazardous to health.

Caffeine addiction can result in mood swings. It certainly has the potential to cause or exacerbate gastrointestinal ailments, heart disease, cancer, kidney disease, psychiatric disorders, and hyperactivity. Withdrawal results in nausea, headaches, and depression.

People who have learned to depend on "filling up" pain or relationship voids with cups of coffee for a short-term "fix" often are more vulnerable to having clusters of other oral addictions – cigarettes, alcohol, and/or food. By filling up on chemicals they can stay in control and avoid facing relationship vacuums. While chemicals certainly differ in terms of their harmful effects, all share one primary function: In an addicted system, their use allows the addict to avoid connecting with others and to cover feelings, thus permitting him or her to remain loyal to the family's rules of shame (staying in control and suppressing feelings).

FOOD ADDICTIONS

Food addictions are perhaps the most difficult to deal with successfully, since we cannot live without food. Bulimics, anorexics, and compulsive overeaters must face their "bars" daily.

Bulimia

Bulimia is a common food addiction, especially in adolescent women. The bulimic is thinness-focused and has a distorted self-image, often feeling fat and constantly obsessing

about weight. Bulimics show a wide range of weights, adding
to diagnostic uncertainty.

Fear brought Joyce into therapy. She confessed that each
night she ate almost 12 large cartons of a popular, low-priced,
sugar-and-cream-filled dessert and then promptly vomited.
She looked emaciated and was physically exhausted and in
need of medical attention. When we questioned her husband
about his knowledge of what was going on, he stated, "Well,
I did realize that she was doing a little snacking at night."
Even though he had found the empty cartons heaped high
in the kitchen, his denial was strong enough to prevent his
questioning her. His denial perpetuated the bulimia.

Bulimia is not only a woman's disease. Many compulsive
male runners and physical fitness "junkies" obsessed with remaining youthful succumb to vomiting so that they can keep
their outer selves fit and handsome. Bulimia in men often
goes undetected because therapists do not think of them as
candidates for bulimia. Bud, a highly successful physician
had been in marital therapy for several months before we
asked him questions about his eating patterns. We knew he
was committed to a disciplined exercise program and was
concerned about health issues. Our cue to ask more questions
came from his "overconcern" with his slender wife's weight
gain of five pounds. After a few queries about *his* eating pattern, he disclosed he was vomiting twice a day but thought
he could control it.

Recently, a bulimic client, Sally, stated that she was afraid
that if she were to give up her role of highly successful student that her parents' marriage would fall apart. In her confusion she stated seriously that she knew that if she were just
thin enough, she would be lovable and her parents would stay
together. Her vomiting was triggered by self-contempt and
shame about her binge-eating. The bingeing-vomiting cycle
maintained the shame, which, in turn, maintained the bulimia. Indeed, when she did go into an inpatient hospital
treatment program, her parents did divorce. Her worst fear
was realized. She then began a recovery program and today
is functioning well in her school and family life.

Anorexia nervosa

The number of self-starving women in our culture grows steadily. Commonly seen in affluent families with daughters aged 13–25, anorexia nervosa has become epidemic in some private high schools.

The anorexic often begins starving gradually with feeding-fasting cycles and an intense craving for sweets. Excessive exercises, depression, and use of laxatives often accompany starvation as the disease progresses. Hyperactivity often becomes the natural pace and, in the disease's most advanced stages, forced vomiting is characteristic.

Shame is prevalent in families of anorectics, since the family rule of "respectability" requires that they appear as an exemplary family to the outside world (Palazzoli, 1978). This façade is the false self of the shame-bound system. Family boundaries are fused, with all family actions dependent on accommodating someone else's perceived needs. Such fusion perpetuates the blame/shame cycle. According to Palazzoli, three characteristics – a perfectionistic, obsessive mother, non-expression of feelings, and fear of being out of control – predominate. These same characteristics exist in the shame-bound family. As in many chemically dependent families, often the father is psychologically absent and the mother focuses her attention on her daughter, hoping to satisfy her esteem needs through her daughter.

One young client, Jean, recently learned about her family's role in her anorexia. At the outset of therapy she described her family as "ideal," and her family life as "just fine if it weren't for me." Later we learned that mother became uncontrollably angry whenever any food preparations did not turn out as planned and once became hysterical when the dog ate a cake. During the course of therapy she also observed that her mother's letters gave full acounts of her home menus and restaurant meals she and her husband ate. Jean had been loyal to the family rule that children can never be angry with parents. With no available relationship with her dad, Jean was loyal to her relationship with her mother; she did not express anger. Since her mother was obsessed with food, she symbolically fought her by starving. To complete the family legacy picture, Jean had married a compulsive overeater. Minuchin et al. (1978) found that the cross-joined relationship between generations helps to maintain the rigidity of the system. The enmeshment and overprotectiveness Minuchin described in the psychosomatic families are evident in "anorectic" families.

Compulsive overeating

Overeating is clearly identifiable because the symptom of obesity is so obvious. Obesity (defined here as being 15 pounds overweight) has become an obsessive concern in our culture. One recent study stated that 34 million Americans are overweight (National Public Radio, June, 1985). The "cures" for obesity are almost as numerous as the "causes." Some researchers attribute this confounding and complex obsession with eating and overweight to simple overeating; others state that it is a chemical maladjustment; still others assert that it is a self-abusing pattern of survival learned in the dysfunctional family, an alternative form of nurturing.

Overeaters use willpower to excess to control their obsessions with food. Some undergo gastrointestinal surgery to "shrink" the storage area; others go so far as to have their mouths wired shut inside. The person with a food addiction will often hide food or eat secretly, feeling remorse and shame after a binge. It is not uncommon to hear people refer to themselves as "chocoholics" or "carboholics." In highly addicted families, control may be exerted and strong defensive rationalizations developed to protect the compulsive overeating. Aging, childbearing, heredity, glandular disorders and lifestyles demanding social eating "excuse" the behavior. While the reasons may vary, the shame remains the same. Compulsive overeaters who maintain their shame by bingeing experience the same split self seen in people with other addictions. The "addict" side of the self acts out while the "other" side of the self judges and criticizes it.

Many of the attempts to solve this problem, including deprivation and fasting, have only led to an increased incidence of anorexia nervosa. When people face eating patterns as challenges – to be managed and controlled – they maintain a built-in release, the bingeing to break the control cycle.

Often the addiction is clearly present in obese clients but family therapists find themselves silent about compulsive overeating, following the family's "no talk" rule about overeating in the family. This collusion with the family's rules prevents family change. Family therapists can ask families what they had previously attempted concerning the food addiction and make referrals to specialized programs.

Currently, multifocused programs are achieving some success. To date, the combination of nutritional analysis, behavioral change, and work with the powerlessness inherent in the compulsivity has yielded the best results.

This pattern of addiction is one of the most difficult to treat or change because abstinence is not the answer. Food is a daily necessity. It cannot, like alcohol, be eliminated from one's life with rewarding consequences and improved health. As families work through their pain, it is not unusual for the shutdown feelings of the overeater to surface and the symptom to diminish as self-respect increases.

Presenting cues that warrant a probe into possible food addictions include extreme thinness or obesity, perfectionism regarding physical appearance, and extremely baggy or tight clothing. Interactional struggles over who controls food in the family, obsessional ritualizing of meals, "forgetfulness" about eating, concern about a family member's irregular or non-nourishing eating patterns, and family reaction to dieting are family dynamic cues. Food and eating issues are often metaphors for underlying relationship issues; family therapists are most successful when they address both the real food behavior and its symbolic function in the family.

SPENDING/SAVING ADDICTIONS

Spending or saving addicts are not always readily identified clinically because we often do not talk openly about money. One family had been in therapy for quite some time before we saw the parents in individual sessions. When we asked, "Just how important is money in your life?" the husband, Jack, stared at us with widened eyes and exclaimed, "Why, money is my God! Nothing else is more important to me!" Although we knew he was obsessed with work (which he justified by his role as a "needed" family physician), we had not made the link between work and money.

Indeed, on inquiring, we discovered that he was an obsessive electronics equipment buyer. He read the advertisements daily and continually traded in equipment and replaced or bought new stereo and electronic equipment. Several times he had told himself that he would stop, to no avail. His wife was very upset by his spending, since they had the financial strains typical of a young family, but she had never breached the subject in their therapy sessions. She grew up in an alcoholic family and had learned the rule of loyalty through denial. Jack stated that he felt ashamed of himself for not living up to his father's expectations and thought that, if he had enough "things" to prove success, his father would think more of him. When he visited his first Spenders Anonymous group, he knew he had found his "home."

Many *compulsive shoppers* admit they do not love to shop, but rather love to *buy*. The shame following a binge often causes shoppers to return their goods, only to turn around and buy another armload. Many clients whose dependency on food and alcohol has lessened pursue self-esteem needs by shopping for clothes, thereby remaining loyal to their external focus for need gratification. Shopping provides instant gratification.

Compulsive gambling has many available outlets, with meccas such as Las Vegas being the most blatant examples of the business done at the expense of addicts. Yet local bingo parlors, race tracks, lotteries, football and baseball betting are constant temptations to compulsive gamblers, whose families often lose all their material goods before the addiction is treated.

Louise and Tom, young parents, came in because Louise felt so badly about her *compulsive stealing* of candy bars and blouses. At one point, a store detective had warned her that if he caught her again she would be taken to the police station and charged with theft. Her husband was as involved as she was; both were diligently attempting to control her addiction. By the time they finally came to therapy, both felt truly out of control.

Compulsive hoarding has many guises. Some hoarders justify buying unneeded bargains to "save for the future" or caseloads of foodstuffs to prepare for that inevitable "rainy day" by blaming their having grown up during the Great Depression. Others seek to gain status and acceptance to "prove" their self-worth by accumulating material goods. One such family came to us in despair after the mother was arrested for embezzling half a million dollars. In subsequent family therapy sessions, she revealed that she thought her aging, successful parents might finally accept her if she became successful enough in their eyes. While this is a drastic example, it does show how, if undiscovered, a pattern developed over the years can seduce the victim into believing that she or he can persist and perhaps not be found out.

Presenting cues for therapists include clients' arguments over money or purchases, and retorts to blaming – "Well, if I'm bad, what about all your shopping trips? We already have three popcorn machines!" Intense shame in response to another's questioning or declarative statements about spending/saving issues can also signal the addiction.

WORK ADDICTION

Work addiction, or "workaholism," is difficult to identify because for so many in our culture it is the model for achieving success and includes financial rewards. A "passion" for work is not always addiction. It may merely be an investment in a stimulating, enjoyable career or job. However, if it replaces personal relationships, and if the person cannot choose to stop concentrating on work projects while away from work, it most likely is considered addiction. It is when a person derives his or her entire self-worth and identity from work that working becomes an addiction.

In fact, most work addicts unconsciously fuse their identity with their work—their role envelops them and they become the role. They display little awareness of the fact that behind the role exists a person. When asked to describe themselves, a high percentage of men typically begin by talking about their paid roles in the world (Gilligan, 1982). In contrast, most women define themselves not by role but by relationship.

Work addiction is not gender-bound, however. Many women are workaholics; that is, their primary relationship or interest in life is work, whether it is housework ("a woman's work is never done") or a career. Role behaviors—whether homemaker or career person—provide a secure place for shame-based people who strive for perfection and simultaneously hide their shame. Long hours can often be justified. Confronting the behavior proves difficult, for who has better reason for working hard than the dedicated obstetrician, the beginning businesswoman struggling to keep the family ship afloat or the mechanic with a large family?

Recent studies of young corporate executives show that those who have used drugs recreationally for years are now using drugs in their executive suites (Flax, 1985). As stress increases, so does their drug use. Indeed, abuse of drugs, especially cocaine and prescription drugs, among executives has become a serious national problem, according to *Fortune* magazine. According to this report (Flax, 1985), the number of high-level executives seeking chemical dependency treatment has increased 100 percent over the past five years. Drug abuse can help to maintain the workaholic's "feeling masterful."

One work addict came to realize that he "worked" at everything—his job, his marriage, his parenting, his home. After his first 12-step group meeting, he said he could not quite believe the thoughts and feelings that surfaced when he stopped pushing and just sat still. He acknowledged how hard he had worked at being the good son, the good student, the good professional, the good husband—and yet still did not feel good enough. In family therapy he was able to tell his parents that he intended to be good enough for himself. By doing so he began to break a major pattern of existing to please others.

One clue to work addiction is the unmanageability of a person's life. For example, a young father addicted to his work sounded quite desperate as he asked for an individual appointment. He said that he was unable to return all his business calls, his thinking had become foggy, and he had made some very poor decisions. His personal life had also become unmanageable; his wife and children missed him and were vocal about his shutting them out. It was clear that his involvement in marital therapy would be of little or no avail until he could work through his compulsive work habits. He acknowledged he was seeking to substitute status for love and knew his marriage was at the breaking point.

Another cue for the therapist involves the reversal of priorities: with work addiction the work is first priority, the family second, and the self third. Many therapists find a 12-step group to work on unmanageability and letting go of control is a most helpful adjunct to therapy.

SEXUAL ADDICTION

Sexual addiction has recently been highlighted through such books as Carnes' *The Sexual Addiction* (1983), television talk shows, and a spreading network of self-help groups, including Sexaholics and Sex Addicts Anonymous. Sexual addiction, with behavioral tones of intimacy, actually is a barrier to intimate relationships.

Compulsive sexual behavior includes compulsive masturbation (often with pornography), voyeurism, extramarital affairs, casual encounters with strangers of same or opposite sex, contact with prostitutes, exhibitionism, and prostitution. Compulsive intercourse is another form of addiction. Bonnie and George had had intercourse within the first hour after they met. Soon married, they had intercourse five to six times daily. In therapy recently, Bonnie explained that she had begun to feel out of control after their children were born. She also stated that her sexual relationship was the one aspect of her life over which she had control. In fact, she had refused to take a drink because she feared losing more control.

A more insidious form of sexual compulsivity is sexualized affection, with children often being the objects. Children have reported the "icky" kisses or weird feelings they experienced with some adult family members who were "apparently" giving them affection, but actually satisfying their own compulsive sexual needs. This area of sexual compulsion sometimes results in sexual abuse. For example, an elementary school teacher came to see us because of her concerns about her strong sexual feelings toward many of the youngsters in her class. A recovering alcoholic, she also was concerned about her compulsive masturbation, which became a daily practice in the children's bathroom at school. She stated she had resolved never to do it again, only to find herself filled with shame and remorse after she failed to keep her promise to herself.

Failed attempts to keep promises are a constant in the sexual addict's life. Some years ago a young woman who felt ashamed of her sexual behavior came to us for help. She said that whenever she was out on a date, she "somehow" ended up in bed, even on a first date, and even if she disliked the man. Her relationships never went beyond sexual contact.

We naively suggested some behavioral changes that she could use to control herself, but she returned to tell us that she had not been able to keep her promise to herself. Once again she felt like a failure and ashamed. We hadn't yet learned about sexual addiction and we told her that when she was serious about therapy, she should come back to see us. We were encouraging her to use willpower to control a process over which she clearly had no control. (If she had reported alcohol abuse, we would have asked her to face her powerlessness.) Several more failures led us to ask in depth about the process of being out of control, i.e., compulsive sexual behavior.

Sometimes sexual addiction takes the form of a series of "intimate friendships," with an emotional affair being owned and dismissed as "only emotional, not physical and therefore okay." These emotional affairs can be just as harmful and destructive as acted-out compulsions. The addict's obsessive thinking and psychological absence affect others in his or her life. For instance, as one man admitted to taking long lunch hours with women "friends," what became obvious to us was his constant planning, obsessing, and fantasizing about the next luncheon. From an outsider's view he seemed to be a man with many friendships; it took a skilled clinician to recognize and ask about his compulsivity and shame.

Most of the Sex Addicts Anonymous members are male, since men have been socialized to be sexual aggressors. Many of those attending Co-Sex Addicts Anonymous (people in relationships with addicts) are women, again reflecting the socialization of women to be "sex objects." The patterns of sex-role development in our culture juxtapose the feminine attributes of nurturing, kindness, tenderness, and passivity, and the masculine attributes of aggressiveness, initiation, and responsibility. This model of psychosocial development fosters dependent relationships and supports the behaviors of the sexually addicted.

Also, the media has supported the "falling in love" approach to relationships. For many young women, a relationship has been a way to achieve a social identity. While males have been more frequently identified as sexual addicts, women are often identified as "relationship junkies." Some women find themselves going from one new relationship to another, valuing intensity over duration. Some of these are not overtly sexual, but emotionally binding. Many people have confused their passionate feelings for love. Author Tennov describes the term "limerence" in referring to intrusive thinking and acute longing for a "limerent object" (1979, p. 71). She points out that limerence is not love, but intense obsessive feelings toward another. She also states that limerence increases when lovers can meet "only infrequently or when there is anger between them." When two limerents meet, they typically experience mutual bliss, followed by dissension. When a limerent pairs with a nonlimerent, the latter eventually feels suffocated and confused. Typically, the limerent ends the relationship because the nonlimerent is not satiated by or as passionate as the limerent partner. The limerent person goes on to seek another limerent object. Although limerence is common in shame-bound people, it is often known to disappear when people develop their own sense of worth and join in relationships with affectional bonding, in which compatible interests, mutual preferences, and working well together form the root system for the relationship.

Sexual addiction patterns are not always clearly identified by therapists; they are often shadowed by seductive or flirtatious behaviors, inappropriate disclosures and/or suspicions about affairs, a history of relationship struggles, and conflicts about intimacy and jealousy.

PHYSICAL AND SEXUAL ABUSE AS ADDICTION

With the nation now acknowledging the high incidence of domestic violence in families and the extensiveness of battering and sexual violence, great emphasis has been placed on treatment and prevention. For a small number of people, this battering is addictive. For others the form of abuse is sexual abuse, including incest.

While many offenders have stopped the abusive behavior in short-term treatment programs as required, for some the compulsion to act out remains. Programs utilizing 12-steps, similar to AA, have provided a "safe place" for these men to work on their recovery from addiction (Mason, 1980).

Incest families are not typically identified as addicted families; yet there is a strong correlation existing between sexual abuse (incest) and chemical dependency. Some treatment programs for adolescent chemical abuse report that up to 75 percent of their female patients are incest victims. The incest family maintains their shame by the abusing father, a denying mother, a powerful victimized and burdened daughter, and the guilt- and fear-ridden siblings.

Today we see more male victims of sexual abuse. When asked why we had seen little of this previously, we recalled that it was perhaps that we did not look for it. The form of the sexual abuse of male children often consists of inappropriate fondling by opposite or same sex family members or friends of the family. After enduring boundary violations of physical and/or sexual abuse, the victim learns to repeat the abuse in the next generation and to form abusing relationships when he leaves the family.

The cycle of addictive behavior must be stopped in order for the pattern to be broken in the next generation. The most successful programs today involve treatment of the entire family, with the acknowledgment that the addiction is present in the system, not just between the abusing family members.

Abuse in the family affects *all* its members, although this is not always readily acknowledged. For example, a therapist had grown up in a family where discipline involved hitting the boys with a belt and lightly reprimanding the girls. She had known the unfairness of the system and yet never realized the degree to which witnessing her brothers' abuse had affected her. One day, in talking with an associate, she asked intently about a physical abuse program for one of her clients. The colleague turned to her and asked, "And where was the abuse in your family?" Standing still, flooded with tears as though she had walked into a minefield of repressed pain, she realized for the first time the feelings imposed by the abuse and pain in her family. Her history, long ago recorded in her affective world, then became available to her and she was ready to face the feelings she had long since repressed. Her logic and family mythology had told her that she was the lucky one – she was not hit – but the pain and abuse in the family belonged to her as well as her brothers. The family shame about the abuse was her shame as well. The child who is not assaulted is also a victim of the shame and denial.

Often the presenting clues for identifying sexual abuse in the family include the silent, sullen, withdrawn child or the defiant child. Excessive loyalty to one parent through a scapegoat role is another indicator, as well as the intrafamily marriages discussed in Chapter 4. Other hints to the therapist include polarization of feelings and children with inappropriate power. Perhaps one of the strongest signals to the clinician is the intuitive knowing or "sensing" of a secret.

As abusers and the children of abuse of all ages face the painful memories, they can claim their rightful dignity.

CODEPENDENCE OR COADDICTION

Since addiction exists between people, and since addiction is the symptom for, as well as an integral part of, the entire system's pain, it is essential to understand the interactional process that has helps sustain the addiction.

"Codependence" refers to the interactional dynamic of shamebound family members that attempts to maintain the homeostasis in the system. A codependent is a family member who has been dependent on the identified person or addict, helping maintain the addiction through focusing on the addict. The codependent engages in denial, control, protection, and minimizing.

Many family-based treatment centers today bring in family members as part of the individual's addiction treatment. A few programs require the entire family's participation in treatment, thereby removing the stigma from the alcoholic or abuser and greatly assisting other family members in accepting that they are in this together. In treatment codependents learn about the overt and covert controlling behaviors that have actively maintained the cycle of shame and addiction.

Due to incomplete boundaries, codependents lack fully trusting selves; their "zippers" are not on their insides. They have learned to rely on external validation for their sense of self-worth. The codependent pattern may take on three styles. The first style involves the "giving away" of the self to accommodate others. In their desire to be accepted and liked, they attempt to please others by agreeing with their thoughts, feelings and behaviors. They automatically respond to others based on what they think they want. They have learned to believe that the split voice of shame is normal; the outer voice states, "Yes, I agree with you," while the inner voice says, "No, I think you're way off on this." The codependency reveals itself in dishonesty in relationships to self and to others – an inability to keep one's word with one's self or with others. Self-hate and shame result from this violation of values. The codependent, in order to cope with the pain of the low esteem resulting from these interactions, puts up fences of protection. Often these defenses are in the form of exaggerated helpfulness, martyrdom, or timidity. Their communication base focuses on agreement/disagreement rather than accuracy or honesty.

A second style for codependents is seen in the "needing to be needed" person. Those who have grown up shutting down their own feelings, often referred to as "adult children," derive their sense of self-worth from taking care of others. They find themselves in supportive and responsible roles. Often they are subtly persuasive with others and have many others "leaning" on them. They may struggle with intimacy however, since they have learned how to be the "big" one in a "big-little" relationship, but not how to show their own vulnerability. Codependents with this style find it difficult to accept help from others or to ask for help; they have learned to "do it alone." Often this form of codependence is difficult to sense because it is blanketed in leadership, reliability and success.

A third style of codependence is the "magnetic" style, in which codependence is like a strip of magnetic tape down the front of the entire self. When such individuals meet others with the same tape, they blur or fuse together, losing themselves in one another's thoughts, feelings and actions. Some have referred to this as their "velcro strip." Those who have grown up in shame-bound families will find others to complement their "magnetic" strip, continuing, through their loyalty, the fused relationships from their past. Intimate relationships are especially difficult because entering any relationship is like stepping on a track; once they step on, they feel helpless about knowing how to get off.

While codependence takes on many forms and can be identified in symptoms of overconcern, manipulation, repression, and delusional thinking, it is not always as ingrained in personality factors as is the dynamic of the addict. One recent study of codependents entering a treatment center with an alcoholic family member showed that over 50 percent of the codependents had normal MMPIs, reflecting their codependence as a coping pattern rather than an identified pathological issue (Williams, 1984). Many codependents have found help through the Adult Children of Alcoholics Groups and other self-help groups (Brown, 1985).

Codependence can occur in any system, not just in biological families. For instance, recently a group of nuns approached us with their concerns about one of their sisters. We began to question the specific participation of the codependents involved in her apparent drug abuse. We learned that one of the sisters (Louise) very actively insisted that the wine leftover after services be given to Sr. Anna. The codependent Louise wielded her power in the community to help Anna remain isolated and well supplied with wine and cigarettes.

In working with the whole "family" of sisters, we learned about Sr. Louise's excessive controlling of Sr. Anna's behavior. Whenever people raised questions about Sr. Anna's drinking, Sr. Louise told them that Anna was "upset" and must not be bothered. A myth was created to protect the secrecy and shame of her addiction. When the sisters gathered together, a few questions led to the unfolding of many stories about painful feelings denied, uneasy personal encounters, and resulting self-doubt. They asked Sr. Anna to go into treatment for her alcoholism. She did so the next day.

The primary codependent, Louise, was even more deluded than Anna, however. She said that she felt badly for Anna and suggested there were obvious reasons for her drinking. She joined Al-Anon and also participated in a family program in a treatment center to learn about her need to have someone dependent on her — her lifelong way of being in relationships.

This family learned that Sr. Anna's chemical abuse could not have existed without their cooperation. They had been loyal to the rules of shame; their obedience vows helped sustain their acceptance and denial. The addiction had affected all their lives. In subsequent interviews several sisters disclosed that they had grown up in alcoholic families and had never thought about their own recovery processes.

Addiction must be treated within the system for greatest efficacy. It is a great struggle for clients completing individual treatment to return to relatively unchanged codependent systems. While support from self-help groups is primary, recovery can be greatly enhanced when all the victims of the addiction work on the recovery together.

The recovery for the coaddict or codependent takes much longer than does the behavioral withdrawal for the person who receives treatment for a specific addiction. In order for codependents to recover, they have to face the feelings they have repressed and their own motivation for "apparently" giving themselves away to so many others in their desire to be loved. This "desire to be loved" has resulted in low self-esteem and fear of intimacy, leading to their own compulsive behaviors toward controlling others. As they learn about self-trust and rebuild their boundaries, they will no longer need others to be dependent on them and, in their separateness, can move toward love and intimacy rather than caretaking and denying.

References

Bach, R. (1977). *Illusions*. New York: Delacourt.

Bowen, M. (1978). *Family therapy in clinical practice*. New York: Jason Aronson.

Brown, S. (1985). *Treating the alcoholic*. New York: John Wiley.

Carnes, P. (1983). *The sexual addiction*. Minneapolis: CompCare Publications.

Coleman, E. (1982). Family intimacy and chemical abuse: The connection. *Journal of Psychoactive Drugs, 14* (1–2), 153–157.

Elkin, M. (1984). *Families under the influence*. New York: Norton.

Flax, S. (1985, June). The executive addict. *Fortune*, 24–31.

Gilligan, C. (1982). *In a different voice*. Cambridge, MA: Harvard University Press.

Goodman, E. (March 29, 1985). Cigarette makers taken to court. *The Boston Globe*.

Mason, M. (1980). The role of the female co-therapist in the male sex offenders group. In: R. Forleo & W. Pacini (Eds.). *Medical sexology*. Littleton, MA: PSG.

Milkman, H. & Sunderwirth, S. (1985). Esalen Catalog (K. Thompson, Ed.). Big Sur, CA.: Esalen.

Minton, J. (1984). Fibrocystic breast disease. In: John L. Cameron (Ed.). *Current surgical therapy*. St. Louis: Mosby.

Minuchin, S. (1974). *Families and family therapy*. Cambridge, MA: Harvard University Press.

Minuchin, S., Rosman, B. & Baker, L. (1978). *Psychosomatic families*. Cambridge, MA: Harvard University Press.

National Public Radio. (June 1985). All things considered. New York.

Palazzoli, M. S. (1978). *Self starvation*. New York: Jason Aronson.

Stanton, M. D. & Todd, T. (1982). *The family therapy of drug abuse and addiction*. New York: Guilford.

Stanton, M. D. (1985). Personal communication.

Tennov, D. (1979). *Love and limerence*. New York: Stein and Day.

Williams, T. (1984). Notes on alcoholism. Unpublished manuscript. Minneapolis: Hazelden.

8

UNDERLYING ASSUMPTIONS OF THE THERAPY PROCESS

As we have explored shame in earlier chapters, we have clarified the foundations of our theoretical framework. Since we use our selves in personal ways when working with shame, our approach to therapy could be described as heuristic – that is, we discover broadening dimensions of our principles, both personal and professional, through our personal involvement with our clients. As we affect our clients, our clients affect us, as well as our relationships in and out of the office. The learning we take from this process helps us to gradually unravel and expand our philosophy of family therapy, which we refer to as "home-brewed epistemology." Our work with shame has demanded a shift in our epistemology.

Several assumptions form the underpinnings of this evolving epistemological base. These assumptions describe the values that form the basis for our work with people; they are the root system from which our therapeutic strategies grow. We recognize that the assumptions listed here are not "new" to the field of therapy; they simply reflect the state of our current thinking.

1) FAMILY SYSTEMS THERAPY IS A MULTILEVEL CONTEXTUAL PROCESS

Our therapy model for shame is inclusive and multilevel – that is, we explore the individual and/or family relationships within three systems: the family of procreation or family in which the client now lives; the family of origin; and the "family" of affiliation (close friendship).

Whether an individual, couple, or family comes for an initial interview, the immediate context we face is the current family. This *family of (pro)creation* can be a biologically united family of two parents and their natural born children or a child-free couple (Hey, 1979). Other family forms include adoptive families, blended ("step")families, homosexual couples with children, or single-parent families. Usually we learn about these relationships in the early stages of therapy, since clients typically identify them in their presenting concerns.

We focus our attention on the *family of origin* because we assume that clients' present behavioral patterns were shaped by parents and siblings and extended family members with whom they grew up. Carl Whitaker (1981) has stated, "There is no such thing as an individual; we are all family fragments." In other words, the person we meet in our office is the culmination of ancient and modern history. To aid us in evaluation we include a family genogram form with our intake form; clients denote their place in their family tree. They also code significant information, such as PA for physical abuse, CMP for chronic medical problems, etc.

We assume that a network of support, of close friendship outside the family system, is vital to a family's health and growth. Often we refer to this network as the *family of affiliation*.

For some people, however, this "family" of affiliation becomes the primary resource for sharing family rituals around significant life events. Shame-bound people who have been cut off from their families of origin have often turned to these "families" of affiliation to meet their needs for family. We often include these "family" members in the therapy.

This family systems model is especially fitting in working with shame because of its "no fault" approach. Clients can see that they are a part of a much larger system and played only one part in the history, that everyone grows up within a family context. This insight can provide relief to the person who has internalized much of the family pain. This can also plant seeds for the essential understanding that we all do belong — that while we are responsible for our behavior today, we did not become who we are alone. One parent's comment to an adult child summed up this relationship clearly: "I know that your problems have my fingerprints on them, but the solution is up to you."

We also remind clients that they can only change themselves, that they cannot change systems. Yet, paradoxically, as individuals change, so do the systems in which they live. It is within in this context that we meet other members of the system. Whether it is the individual as client or the family as client, we explore the three family contexts.

The model for our multilevel growth approach is nonlinear and can best be seen as a helix — a model of continuity and connection and correction, with spirals dipping downward into the past and integrating the demythified history into the present. This family process is never complete, just as we are never complete. Growth is an ongoing, dynamic, integrative process of change.

2) THERAPY IS AN ONGOING PROCESS

Two major areas come to mind when we explain that therapy is an ongoing process. The first is our bias toward a family life-cycle approach, and the second is our attitude toward change.

Family life-cycle approach

We can more readily identify the beginning of therapy than we can mark its ending, because the process often continues over time, sometimes over the life-cycle of the family *and* the therapist. For example, we often work with a couple on their marital relationship and later get a telephone call asking for help with parenting issues concerning an adolescent child, and then again with aging issues and the death of parents.

After terminating the original therapy contract, the therapist can shift to the role of family consultant, just as physicians, lawyers, dentists, and clergy are involved in families' lives. We often work with an "open door" policy – with the understanding that a family can return at some later date as other developmental issues appear. Also, since we acknowledge a growth model, we know that there is no one fixed outcome or "cure" in what we do.

An example of working with family members of all ages and at all phases in the life-cycle involves Jan and Steve, who entered therapy to work on their new and second marriage. During that work their blended families met for a few interviews (with former spouses and their mates and their children). At yet another stage in their lives they brought in their adolescent children for conflict resolution. Most recently Steve, 45, brought in his 85-year-old mother and his 60-year-old brother; before his mother died he wanted to learn more about his blurred family history and his early years in the family. As a result of their family sessions, Steve, his mother, and his brother divulged family secrets and broke through strict prohibitions against expressing their love. They learned new patterns for expressing their feelings to one another. They talked openly about mother's dying and death and heard her requests regarding burial. Recently Steve called to tell us that his mother had died and that he and his brother were together, holding her hands when she was dying. Their family request to us was that we continue to bring in parents of adults, stating, "It is never too late."

First-order versus second-order change

Our premise about change lies in our acknowledging that, when people come to us with problems or "stuckness," they may be seeking symptom relief. For example, a couple entered therapy in pain and distress because an extramarital affair had been revealed. In the initial interview the man agreed to stop seeing the other woman. Although this change occurred within the system, the system itself remained unchanged, an example of *first-order change* (Watzlawick, Weakland, & Fisch, 1974). This behavioral change gave symptom relief and could be described as a brief therapy intervention. The couple then contracted for further therapy involving exploration of their marital dynamics. In this part of their therapy, they learned about their loyalty to their family-of-origin rules and involved both sets of parents in their therapy. This longer-term therapy resulted in what we described as *second-order change*, since they experienced change in the "body of rules governing their structure or internal order" (Watzlawick et al., 1974).

We assume that the beginning stage of therapy often involves first-order change. As trust deepens and clients reveal themselves and their secrets and unravel distortions in their family histories, they can make choices that move them toward second-order change. It is this second-order change which, as it weaves its color into the family life-cycle at its different stages, contributes to and enriches therapy as a lifelong process.

3) THE FAMILY UNCONSCIOUS IS UNLOCKED

Carl Whitaker has stated: "I am firmly convinced that members of the same family read each other in great detail and that most of that information never reaches consciousness" (Taub-Bynum, 1984).

Just as each family member has an unconscious, so too does the family. Taub-Bynum describes the "family unconscious" as "in a sense between the personal and collective regions of the psyche" (1984, p. 10). He distinguishes the *family unconscious* from the *collective unconscious* of Carl Jung's "inherited faculty of the psyche" in its "shared images, experiences, and roles held in common by the members of the family matrix. The family unconscious constitutes a shared emotional field and matrix of consciousness" (Taub-Bynum, 1984, p. 11). It is this concept which helps explain the inheritance of shame or recurrent psychosomatic illnesses through several generations.

Clients often experience the family unconscious when they face family "coincidences." For example, a woman came to

therapy feeling very discouraged about the cut-offs in her
family of origin. She had not heard from any family members
in almost six years and had decided that the time had come
for her to resolve her feelings about unresolved family pain
"once and for all." During her second interview, she exclaimed
that she was uncertain about just what to think about the
four independent, individual telephone calls she had just received from her out-of-state siblings, as well as from one
parent – all for no apparent reason. The fine line between coin-
cidence and the family's unconscious plot both surprises and
confounds us at times.

Duke Stanton (Stanton & Todd, 1982, p. 21), in his work
with substance abusers, also discerns "family unconscious
plots," as storylines being played out in a drama written by
the collective unconscious of the family, with imminent danger of something occurring (death and/or destruction included)
at an unconscious level. A family member could receive the
unconscious message, "If you have to separate, then there is
one way you can do it and that is by dying."

We see another expression of the family unconscious when
a shameful secret is revealed. It is quite common to hear family members state that they "knew it at some level."

When people seek therapy they have a concrete awareness
of their problems and pain; however, many dimensions of the
therapy lie outside the conscious awareness of family members. Therapist(s) and clients are surprised when they find unconscious information made available to them. As people
state their goals and work toward achieving consciously desired
changes, they often reach a point where they reflectively
state, "Now I know why I really came." That unconscious
motivation, which is not identified by language, becomes
available to clients during the therapy. Family therapist Anita
Whitaker (1983) states it clearly: "I guess we're all on automatic pilot."

4) WE DON'T ACCEPT CLIENTS' DENIAL
AS OUR REALITY

In the initial stages of therapy we attempt to follow clients'
perceptions of their reality but often see their delusion and

denial of shame. Members of the shame-bound family, with its affective shutdowns, typically have been living the delusional myths it created to survive. These myths are born out of loyalty to family rules – the rules governing the interactional patterns of shame. In order not to talk about real experience, the family creates myths to explain its reality and typically presents some delusional thinking about what is "normal."

We accept the role of presenting our own mirroring about what we hear and see, breaking family rules by commenting on our own reality. For example, the adult who was physically abused in childhood learns (through denial and minimizing) to accept battering inflicted by his or her spouse. We frequently hear the comment, "Well, it only happens when I make him (or her) angry." In *Prisoners of Childhood*, Alice Miller discusses the affective cut-offs of children who have learned to take care of their parents' pain. Given this shutdown of their emotional responses, children have not been able to develop their affect, leading to distortions in perceptions. This dynamic results in developmental arrest; in therapy they return to revisit this shutdown and reclaim buried feelings.

We present different views in response to clients' realities. Thus, clients have an opportunity to react to and talk about differentness – a first step in acknowledging individuation. This approach acknowledges differentness as natural and normal and moves clients to take steps toward identifying their own belief systems. We point out that the two of us do not have to think alike. During this crucial stage we assume that the therapist will accept clients where they are, respecting their pain and offering empathic support. Our policy is to not take down "fences" (defenses) until we know what purpose they serve. We presume that many clients, just like many of us, have grown up with family myths that have led to dysfunctional patterns of relating. Our goal, in the early stages of therapy, is not to confront, but to work with the clients as they clarify their own perceptions by reclaiming buried affect.

As clients begin to trust and allow their vulnerability to

surface, they are able to restructure their own cognitive and affective perceptions. In turn, they identify values and stand up for their perceptions. In the final stages of therapy, the relationship shifts from the foster-parenting imbalance to a more balanced relationship in which the therapist follows the client's perceptions.

As we follow and reflect our own perceptions, we find it important to have available outside consultation. We strive to be clear about our own issues so that they do not color our pictures of reality, and to stay humble about our definition of reality. We often tell our clients that we cannot promise to be *right*, but we do promise to be *honest* about what we see and hear.

5) THE SELF IS USED AS THE TECHNIQUE

The relationship established between the therapist and client is the most powerful element in the process of therapy. Trust is primary to this relationship; authenticity is primary to trust. Trust is not founded on words.

We define trust as "the reliance upon the nonverbal communication of another person in order to achieve a desired but uncertain goal in a risky situation" (Giffin, 1967). We believe that as clients experience their pain and work through shame in a safe setting, their trust deepens and they come to believe that their therapists will walk with them.

In using ourselves we are aware that the generational line between therapist and client must be clearly defined. Because of boundary confusion in their history, clients facing shame are vulnerable to misinterpreting friendly gestures such as having lunch or giving a ride home at the end of the day. When clients are working through their shame-related issues, an imbalance of power exists in the therapist-client relationship; the therapist must be in charge of setting limits and maintaining boundary clarity.

As we focus on developing trust we use metaphors to help us keep this relationship clearly defined. These metaphors remind both our clients and ourselves that this is a symbolic relationship.

One metaphor we often use is that of coach (Whitaker, 1974). As coaches we can be there to support the team, or the player, yet we cannot "play" for them. David Keith (1985) has also used the swimming coach metaphor to describe co-ther- py, with "one coaching from the edge of the pool and the other getting in the water" (Keith, 1985).

Another common metaphor is that of foster parent, in which we assume that we will be supportive of the person's or family's growth for a given period, and that we will enter their lives and they ours for a specified time. While the rela- tionship remains forever in history, the work together is time- limited.

The foster parent metaphor is as helpful to the therapist as to the client. When we use ourselves so personally with our clients, it is important to be clear about the distinction be- tween foster parent and real parent, especially when the client is focusing on developmental issues and seeking a "loving parent." We cannot promise to be available for a whole life- time or as a real parent. We are there specifically for the task of "working our way out of a job."

In addition to clarifying boundaries, such metaphors can help the family experiment with a more abstract perspective. We also use metaphors to enter clients' worlds, such as talking about "sowing, weeding and harvesting" with a farm family. When we enter their worlds through metaphor we also in- crease ambiguity by permitting confusion to surface. Confu- sion can be useful to a perfection-seeking family. For example, an accountant became aware of discrepancies in the family ledger when we referred to "things not adding up quite right."

FATHER: Other than Jane's eating disorder, there are no prob- lems in our family.
THERAPIST: But your wife says that she is depressed. And you said earlier that you were concerned about your drinking. When I add up all the things I've heard today, my bottom line is different from yours. You add this all

up to "no problems," but I see some pretty troubled people. Do you know what it means to "fudge the figures"?
FATHER: (Looking confused and a little surprised) Sure . . .
THERAPIST: Do you suppose you might be fudging the figures
   when you talk about the family, making the bottom line
   look better than it actually is?

The father, as well as other family members, could then more
fully accept the confusion about their own family life by
transferring the metaphoric language to their patterns of daily living.

No matter what style a therapist uses or how creatively
he or she connects with a family, the deciding factor in establishing a solid relationship is the caring with which it unfolds.

6) FAMILY INTIMACY IS AN UNSPOKEN
GOAL

Our definition of family intimacy is *the experience of closeness and familiarity between two or more family members in
a variety of contexts, with the expectation that the experience
and the relationship will persist over time.*

Shame, with its interpersonal breakdowns (Kaufman, 1985),
is a barrier to intimacy. Owing to secrets and low self-esteem,
most people in shame feel lonely and isolated. We assume
that as people work through shame, they will find greater intimacy in all relationships. While family living holds the *potential* for intimacy, the process is cyclical and intermittent.
Intimate relationships involve antagonism and hostility as
well as loving. Intimate relationships provide more occasions
for conflict, and conflict between intimates is usually more
intense. In addition, intimacy needs and expressions vary
over the life-cycle.

For shame-bound people who have experienced fusion and
invasion masked as "closeness," becoming intimate is frightening. Those who have experienced sexualized affection must
relearn about caring affection. We respect that the developmental affective age of clients is quite often much younger

than their chronological age and work with them at that "felt" age.

Respect for ethnicity is germane to the therapy process and the move toward increased intimacy. Closeness in Italian and Greek families may look quite different from closeness in Scandinavian families.

One of the "unconscious desires" mentioned earlier in this chapter is the natural desire for family closeness. In many families this closeness is experienced not in feeling language, but rather in work, recreation, storytelling, quiet reading together, or even fighting. We remind clients not to impose their rules of intimacy on their parents' generation, telling them that some visits home may resemble anthropological field trips.

7) FAMILY THERAPY IS A SPIRITUAL JOURNEY

Shame erodes the spirit, that natural, animating life force that is unknown to human language. Spirit is made up of mind, the unconscious, and intuition. Families as well as individuals are spiritual. We do not mean religious when we say spiritual, although some people have known their spirituality through religion.

As clients face their shame, their spirits awaken and resume their natural growth. One client stated, during her closing session in therapy, "I used to plan my life and now I just show up!" This was her shorthand way of stating that she was now able to trust life.

Trusting life comes from making some meaning of who we are, what we are all about. When we confront shame, we become aware of emptiness, a spiritual hunger. Our attempts to fill this hunger with controlling, compulsive behaviors only lead to pain and remorse. Carl Jung was aware of this compulsive "filling of the void." He wrote to Bill Wilson, the cofounder of AA, saying that he thought alcoholism was the search for wholeness, for a "union with God" (1974).

We have found that 12-step support systems (e.g., Alcoholics Anonymous, Al-Anon, Sex Addicts Anonymous, Co-

SAA, Overeaters Anonymous, and Gamblers Anonymous) are important adjuncts for continued spiritual growth. These groups help members to focus on "letting go" and accepting their powerlessness over external events and over the behavior of others.

Compulsive, addictive behaviors are one way of facing our spiritual dimension; crises are another. Families often face their shame through crises. We believe that when families seek help for their crises, they are at some level facing a possible "gift."

Chinese writers have long talked about crisis as "danger" and "opportunity." The two characters from the written Chinese language are Wei (danger), a face-to-face encounter with a powerful animal, and Chi (opportunity), the blueprint of the universe (Huang, 1983). Families who come to us in crisis face an opportunity for change and growth. In this sense, we believe that crises are functional in the spiritual development of a family, that they shift the family's perspective.

This possibility for growth also involves what Carl Whitaker has called "energy conversion." One example of this is unexpressed anger converted to random motor behavior or compulsive work. Any time energy conversion occurs, we have more energy available for work. He reminds us that we are connected in all our systems — skeletal, anatomical, affective, physiological. This "conversion" is often seen in therapy when hurt behind anger surfaces with the falling away of controlling, defensive behaviors. With this change to vulnerability and exposure, people express themselves more freely and congruently and deeper emotional connections are possible. This "conversion" of energy also affects the therapist, paving the way toward what Whitaker refers to as an "authentic therapeutic encounter."

In talking with families about their channel for their natural spirituality, we often use the "clogged drain" metaphor. We tell families that all the "gunky stuff" has to come out and float to the surface before the drain can again flow freely. Families find that the hurt, anger and rage known in shame, which were felt and never expressed over the years, are often buried under repression and denial. These built-up layers of accumulated pain so clog our "spiritual drains" that release is demanded by our internal systems. We often refer to family therapy as "Drano." With Drano and a willing family, the "drains" can be unclogged to allow the family's natural human feelings to surface.

Although we believe in the opportunity for growth and closeness, we do not assume that there is any lockstep pattern leading to family closeness. We assume failure – both theirs and ours – to be part of the process; we assume resistance. In many families, we must confront the family's unconscious plot, in which one member serves as the vehicle for another's self-destruction.

We acknowledge that family life involves suffering. Our helix model of growth is recursive. As we work with families in pain and crises, threads from the old fabric are woven into the new, creating new patterns in the spiritual cloth of the family. We often see a deepening of compassion, a softening toward others, and acceptance and respect of others' separateness.

8) THERAPISTS GROW FROM A PERSONAL APPROACH

In discussing family therapy, Carl Whitaker said, "You can teach what it is; you can teach how to *do* it – you can never teach how to *be* it." We assume that therapists who engage personally in their work with clients' shame are seeking their own personal growth. We also take risks when our clients are working on some of the same issues as we are, pushing our depths and our integrity through respect and care in these relationships. For us family therapy is a path to becoming more humble that is fraught with ambiguity, surprises and failures. By working personally with clients, therapists grow in four areas: dealing with transference issues; recognizing their own unfinished business; making use of consultation; and building support groups.

In the early stages of their growth, therapists commonly react to clients' *transference issues*. Therapists' (as well as clients') boundaries are strengthened when therapists practice limit-setting and acknowledgment of projections in daily work with families. When therapists work with shame, they are subject to facing more of their own shame, a reminder that we are never completely "finished" as human beings.

Therapists' own *unresolved issues* provide the upsets necessary for their growth. By exploring our own issues, we as therapists can face ghosts and our own unfinished family business.

In our supervision groups therapists work with clients with whom they feel stuck. A therapist may invite the family or couple to the supervision group, where the group can sit in the same room and observe his or her nonverbal as well as verbal behaviors and give feedback. Often the stuckness is related to some unfinished business from the family of origin or of (pro)creation.

Lynn, a member of the supervision group, brought in a couple with whom she felt stuck and angry. She reported getting into struggles with the husband, and recognized that she was probably fighting him in place of his wife, who had not yet stood up to him. The group told Lynn that they saw her as simultaneously angry with and protective of the wife. Later they questioned her about where she had felt like that before. Lynn, with tear-filled eyes, acknowledged that the wife reminded her of her younger sister, whom Lynn protected for years. Lynn had never told her sister how upset she was about her sister's constant backing away from any conflict with their parents, leaving it up to Lynn. Lynn now met her unfinished business with her sister in the office.

Consultation is a vital aspect of therapy. If we do not consult with others, we are subject to deluding ourselves. In a supportive consultation environment, whether in-house or out-of-office, therapists can learn about their own epistemology and become more aware of their own "missing pieces."

Therapists also meet their life-cycle issues in therapy. Having a safe consultation system in which these issues can surface is essential. Therapists who have recently experienced divorce or other losses, such as children's leaving home or a family member's death or sickness, are much more vulnerable in their professional roles. As we remove our blinders and face our life-cycle events, we are better able to use ourselves in working with clients.

The *support group* may or may not be found in the consultation group, but it is essential to prevent burnout, as well as to provide for self-care. Empathic responses from colleagues and friends are essential if therapists are to perform at their best. When therapists face families in shame, a good deal of honest emotional expression involving intense feelings surface. The painful stories and human revelations heard in the therapy room may be absorbed at some level by the therapist. It is especially hazardous for a therapist in private practice to work in isolation.

A supportive staff of co-workers can prove invaluable. The roles of administrator, receptionist, and other team members or partners are essential to the health and strength of the system. The realization that we are supported by people who believe in us can give us the strength to do whatever we feel is necessary.

9) A HUMAN APPROACH IS A FEMINIST APPROACH

We assume that we work as feminist therapists—that is, we are committed to respecting people as human beings, not as culturally stereotyped males and females. In systems theory training we accepted the concept of complementarity; since then we have been painfully making ourselves aware that we must view the family systems we experience in the context of the greater sociopolitical system—that of power imbalance and patriarchy. We believe it is through a feminist approach that we can grow by facing our own challenges and inherited cultural biases.

We include in our approach the concept of gender privilege. By this we refer to therapist and client sharing a cultural socialization. A female therapist can often start from a base of similar and shared societal history when working with a woman who has been violated sexually, whether in the past or present, in or out of a relationship. The converse is true for the male therapist who has known particularly male struggles, such as the push to be athletic and aggressive or the victimization involved in "parent-child marriages" or sexual abuse.

Some seductive people (either clients or therapists) state they are more "comfortable" working with the opposite gender; this does not necessarily mean that they are well served. People with boundary confusion do not have the common sense needed to set limits and form identity *and* relationship boundaries.

As both men and women reveal themselves to us, feminist issues are expressed more openly. We offer men's groups and women's groups as adjuncts to therapy. Since shame is not gender-bound, working with shame provides a fertile field for people to become more fully human. As we witness the honesty behind masks, we all benefit by recognizing that beyond our roles we are persons.

References

Framo, J. (1976). Family of origin as a therapeutic resource for adults in marital and family therapy: You can and should go home again. *Family Process, 15,* 193–210.

Giffin, K. (1967). The contribution of studies of source credibility to a theory of interpersonal trust in the communication process. *Psychological Bulletin, 68,* p.000.

Hey, R. (1979). Social structure of the family. Lecture, University of Minnesota, Minneapolis.

Huang, C. (1983). *Quantum soup.* New York: Dutton.

Jung, C. G. (1928). The concept of the collective unconscious. In: R. F. C. Hull (Trans.). *Archetypes and the collective unconscious, collected works.* Bollingen Series XX. Princeton, NJ: Princeton University Press.

Jung, C. (1974). *Letters.* In: Bollingen Series XCV. (R.F.C. Hull. Trans. & Ed.). Princeton, NJ: Princeton University Press.

Kaufman, G. (1985). *Shame* (2nd ed.). Cambridge, MA: Schenkman Publishing.

Keith, D. (January, 1985). Conversation with author. St. Paul, MN.

Miller, A. (1981). *Prisoners of childhood.* New York: Basic Books.

Stanton, M. D. & Todd, T. (1982). *The family therapy of drug abuse and addiction.* New York: Guilford.

Taub-Bynum, E. B. (1984). *The family unconscious.* Wheaton, IL: Theosophical Publishing.

Watzlawick, P., Weakland, J., & Fisch, R. (1974). *Change: Principles of problem formation and problem resolution.* New York: Norton.

Whitaker, A. (March 1983). Conversation. Carmel, CA.

Whitaker, C. (1984). Personal conversation. St. Paul, MN.

Whitaker, C., & Malone, T. (1981). *The roots of psychotherapy.* New York: Brunner/Mazel.

Williamson, D. S. (1981). Personal authority via termination of the intergenerational hierarchical boundary: A "new" stage in the family life cycle. *Journal of Marriage and the Family, 7,* 451–452.

9

MOVING FROM
SHAME TO RESPECT

Before we can be effective as therapists, we must wrestle
with the problem of how to escape the paradox of control. It
is not easy for either therapists or clients to move out of the
sphere of influence of the shame system. From the control-
oriented perspective of this system, therapists want to be
successful and show results, and clients often expect therapy
to produce a "fix," a cure in the form of a secure state of well-
being. Of course, this is not life. But what do we therapists
expect therapy to achieve? Life is a process. Therapy can
restore a healthy process of dealing with life even if it cannot create a securely controlled state of health. When therapists accept that principle it helps liberate them from the
control trap.

When people ask for therapy, they usually aren't asking
for a change in their system. They want help with a specific
problem in living, such as a school behavior problem in a
child, or marital discord, or depression. As family therapists
we take the specific problem of concern and try to understand
it by placing it in the larger context of the family system. We
ask, "How does the family system interact with this particular problem?" "How does this system (with its network of
relationships, communication patterns, and history) produce
the particular problem at hand?" Furthermore, we ask, "How
does this particular problem maintain the system?" Indeed,
it is the latter question which points to many of the ther-

apeutic methods used with shame-bound families. A therapist working with shame will focus less upon changing the system to relieve the symptom and more upon understanding and deciphering how the symptom may be part of the central organizing loyalties which keep the system stuck.

THE INITIAL PHASE
OF THERAPY

Therapy begins with the first request for help, whether it comes by telephone or in person. It includes the development of a therapeutic contract between clients and therapist, and evaluation of the system's dynamics and several therapeutic interventions. This phase may last up to ten sessions and in many cases constitutes the whole therapeutic experience. It is synonymous with much of what is called brief therapy. Very often symptomatic improvement occurs in this phase of family therapy, and the initial goals of the clients are reached.

When the first contact occurs with a potential client (by telephone in our practice), we ask for specific information about the problem at hand. We do not schedule an appointment simply because someone asks for it. We need to know more than the problem itself. We need to know the *context* surrounding this problem in order to get some sense of the system. What specific event led to this request for therapy and who are the family members in this person's life? That information is necessary to plan who will be asked to come to the first session. The initial call and the arrangement for the first session are the beginning of therapy. A telephone intake is never a clerical or routine function artificially set off from therapy.

CLIENT: I would like to make an appointment to see you.
THERAPIST: What made you decide you wanted therapy at this time?
CLIENT: Well, I've been having some difficulties lately and my sister said you were the therapist her friend saw.

Comment: Already in the first three sentences the therapeutic dialogue is taking form. The therapist is asking for information to place this request for therapy into a context. The client's reply remains vague about the problem. The therapist's main task at this stage is to lay the first foundation stones for a successful therapeutic outcome. That will be done by knowing in advance who is in the system and designing an entry which begins with a relationship to the whole rather than with an alignment with one member. Therefore, it is important to press for the needed information (to the extent that it can be comfortably conveyed in this first contact).

THERAPIST: Can you give me some idea of the kind of difficulties you've been having?

CLIENT: I've been pretty depressed for a while and I'm really unhappy in my marriage. One of the things I'm thinking about is whether or not to stay married.

THERAPIST: I think we could work something out for an appointment, but first I need some more information from you. Can you tell me who all lives with you in your household?

CLIENT: There's just me and my husband and my six-year-old son.

THERAPIST: Do they know you have been so unhappy?

CLIENT: I'm sure they can feel it in some ways, but my husband doesn't pick up on things like that very much.

THERAPIST: What does your husband think about getting therapy?

CLIENT: It's fine with him if that's what I want to do, as long as it doesn't involve him.

Comment: We now have a basic outline of the membership in this family and some preliminary impressions that the marital relationship is on the disengaged side. What we still need is the specific event which brought this woman to the point of seeking therapy. While we do not press individuals to reveal more than they are comfortable telling on the telephone, knowing the precipitating event reveals something

about the nature of the system and what is hurting enough
to produce this request.

THERAPIST: It sounds like you've been unhappy for some time.
Can you tell me what was the final straw that motivated
you to make this call?

CLIENT: Yes, it was spending a miserable weekend with my
family. The three of us took a long weekend at a cabin
on a lake and it was so hard for me to be around my husband for that long that I got really depressed. I just
hated the whole time there and when we came home
yesterday — well, I knew that I had to do something.

Comment: Apparently increased contact between this woman and her husband intensified her pain to the point of
motivating her request for therapy. This does not tell us
much more than that the marital relationship is currently a
focal point of pain in the system. The therapist decides that
an entry point to the system that will maintain the greatest
number of options for therapeutic decisions would be to ask
the husband and wife to come in together for the first session.

THERAPIST: I would like to set the first session with you and
your husband.

CLIENT: I really don't think he would go in with me and I
don't even care to ask him because he's not that involved
in my problems.

THERAPIST: The way I know of to help you best would be to
bring him along, at least for the first session. After that
we can make plans based on what makes sense, including
the possibility of individual sessions. But I have learned
that it helps the future of your therapy if we have him
here for the first meeting. Would he come along for your
therapy?

CLIENT: OK. How about if we set an appointment and if I
can get him to come along I will. Otherwise I'll come
alone.

THERAPIST: No. I would rather that we set an appointment

for the two of you. If it turns out that it's not going to
work for both of you, I'd like you to give me a call. Then
we can discuss the situation as it stands at that time.
If your husband wants to ask me why I'm inviting him
to come along or what I'm up to, have him give me a call.
CLIENT: OK. I will talk it over with him.

Comment: Now the therapist has arranged a beginning in
therapy which makes it possible to start with a relationship
to the system. This telephone contact is the first stage in
developing a therapeutic contract. The six-year-old child is
not included here but his inclusion later remains an option.
If the child was older or if he was the focus of family pain,
he would have been included from the beginning. A family
therapist needs to enter the system relating to the whole and
validating the relationship within the system. After establishing the therapist's allegiance to the well-being of everyone
in the family, it is possible and often advantageous to see
subgroups or individuals for some of the work.

The initial stage of therapy, beyond the telephone intake,
has many important functions. It includes getting the relevant people together to talk about their concerns, taking a
history of the problem and their attempts to deal with it, and
taking a history of the family system in this generation and
in the past. Reframing of the problem to help people see their
concerns in a different light and strategic interventions to
shift the structure and politics of the family are important
interventions here.

Any of these experiences can produce dramatic relief for
people in their lives, sometimes very quickly. Just getting
people together and talking openly about the problem can
change the context of the problem enough to be of great help.

The precipitating event, the original problem of concern,
needs to be kept in clear view. It is what provides legitimacy
for the therapist's entry into the family and therefore needs
to be incorporated explicitly into the therapeutic contract.

THERAPIST: You've been telling me today, Ann, about how
    you were getting increasingly depressed over the last

few months. And you, Phil, didn't really notice anything different was happening with her. How is it that something so painful was happening to your intimate partner and you didn't know about it?

PHIL: Well, I guess I've had my things to worry about and figured she'd take care of hers.

THERAPIST: Is that how things went in your family when you grew up?

PHIL: Oh yeah. Nobody ever had time to worry about us kids and we pretty much fended for ourselves.

THERAPIST: It seems to me that in trying to help with what's going on in your family today, it would be worthwhile to take a look at how each of you learned to be close to someone else. Does that feel like a helpful direction to you?

PHIL: I guess it does to me because I never really have been that close to anyone.

Comment: In this abbreviated dialogue from a first interview, the therapeutic contract has begun to evolve. It encompasses both a grounding in the pain which brought them into therapy and a systemic response.

History-taking also widens or opens the context. We may take a detailed relationship history when that is relevant to the problem. This places a current relationship problem within a long-term systemic context. In a relationship history we explore the earliest memories a client has of feeling close or important to someone and feeling that there was a genuine exchange of caring or significance. We look for lifetime patterns of reliability, rapport, dignity and respect, abuse, loss and grief. We look at them with parents, siblings, same sex and opposite sex friendships, and sexual relationships. We ask about experiences in intimate and enhancing relationships. It is important to explore abandonments, neglect, and cut-offs of previously vital relationships, because they are usually generated by someone's shame and produce shame in the people involved. What rules and patterns do the family members have for dealing with conflict and with tension? Does conflict occur openly? If it does, are there ways of resolving it?

Other history-taking can be immensely valuable in identifying the sources of shame. In general we first check out
any current shame-maintaining behaviors. If it is relevant we
explore any one of a number of detailed histories: sexual, drug
and alcohol, food and fasting, money use and abuse, physical
abuse. In each of these areas we explore the person's *development of a relationship* to the substance or behavior in question. We begin by asking clients about their earliest experiences in childhood within their own family and outside the
family. We ask about what they saw of their parents' relationship to these substances or behaviors and what they may
know in this regard of other family members (aunts and uncles,
grandparents). They are asked to fill out a genogram form,
making notations about these significant family issues. We
look for experiences of having been badly treated, overstim-
ulated, or given conflicting messages about these substances
and behaviors. As the history reviews one's lifetime, we look
for changes over time in the relationship to the substance or
behavior in question. Has the relationship become dependent
as a *means to control painful feelings, tension, or insecurity*?
When a pattern of dependency and control is found, it is expected to impede or block the ongoing maturational process;
in its place we find rigid or ineffective coping responses and
distressed personal relationships.

When these patterns are found, the relationship can be explored further by clearly, explicitly and unequivocally stopping the behavior. If this is an addictive relationship, we do
not expect a person to be aware that it is so, and we expect
resistance to giving it up, even temporarily, although individuals vary. The *experience* of doing without a behavior or
substance can be extremely enlightening.

Denial and lack of insight are pervasive at this early stage
and a trusting relationship with the therapist is essential.
When a person's central organizing loyalties and means of
controlling and dealing with his or her experience are chal-
lenged, he or she needs to borrow the therapist's belief or con-
viction that this interpretation makes sense. That requires
a willingness to trust. For this reason it is wise for a therapist

to use good judgment in challenging dependency issues with clients. Sometimes the trust allows for strong demands from a therapist; in other instances it does not. We do know that lasting systemic changes do not occur until after primary dependencies have been given up.

We explore old experiences of abuse and boundary invasions in the history-taking and relate them to current life issues. These too are surrounded by denial. People tend to dissociate their feelings of shame and disqualification from the original boundary invasions and traumatic events. They feel badly about themselves and feel unworthy but do not associate those feelings to the injustices and indignities they suffered.

For instance, one man came to therapy after the breakup of his third marriage. He asked for help with his depression. This person's childhood had been spent as the "special child" of an alcoholic mother. He had often been frightened by finding her passed out on the floor in the evening. He would then call an ambulance, not really understanding what was wrong and worrying that his mother might die. In her neediness she would daily turn to him for comforts like rubbing her back, fixing her drinks, listening to her problems.

Now, in adulthood, this man found himself repeatedly entering relationships with women where he was the caretaker. While it would start out as a comfortable relationship, the pattern always evolved into an angry, bitter assaultive one. Each of his wives had become rageful at how controlling he was, and he responded to each by trying harder to please them. He absorbed their anger as the simple result of his own inadequacies, because he had never learned how to engage in a more equal relationship. When he first described his relationship with his mother, he had no awareness of the parent-child role shift. That awareness came from the therapist's actively pointing to the discrepancies. In the process this man found old feelings of injustice and anger that had been denied through out his adult life.

Sometimes simple education and instruction can be helpful in making the connection between shame and one's history.

Many times affect about an early life trauma is totally absent. The therapy then begins with recontacting the old affect and dealing with it as relevant and meaningful from current perspective.

Therapeutically we ask these people, "How did you learn to be so ashamed?" This question undermines the shame at two levels. On the first level is the release that comes when we reassociate feelings of shame with the specific memories of personal harm. On the second level, in the act of searching for the learning, a person takes on the definition of shame as "acquired" rather than "inherent." This is contradictory to the whole shame experience, because shame is felt as fundamental to one's identity. In effect, a person can hardly look for how he or she *learned* to feel ashamed and *feel* ashamed at the same time.

Another useful awareness for a therapist is the fact that painful feelings like grief, rejection, or anger are often first experienced as shame or are covered by a shame response. When that is happening, a therapist can reframe the client's experience with a statement like, "You're grieving the loss you've had and feeling ashamed. Do you think it's not OK to feel pain instead?"

The provocation to reject is a common event in work with shame-bound clients. They universally expect to be rejected and that expectation must always be dealt with on some level. Often the therapist's honest verbal statements that he or she will continue to be available for the work are all that's needed. Some people have learned to use rejection compulsively, as a way to keep control of their lives. As soon as it seems that the therapeutic relationship might have some significance, they engage in provocative behavior oriented toward getting themselves ejected from therapy. The therapist here must walk a fine line between, on the one hand, understanding the behavior as an attempt to precipitate the inevitable, and on the other hand, maintaining limits that will allow therapy to continue.

One client, for instance, insisted on his freedom to smoke in the session, a liberty we do not allow because of our own personal preferences. When he persisted, we terminated the session and he went home saying he'd never be back. As he left we felt the personal temptation to either react with a reciprocal rejection or minimize the limit and find a way around it. We remained emotionally separate from his provocation and said we found him to be a likable person but could not accept his smoke and if he wished he could call back to continue therapy later. We held the limit without rejecting him. He called back two days later, ready to resume his therapy.

These interventions and history explorations may take place in the first few sessions of therapy and produce the relief or change that the clients are seeking. At this point many people will end a successful experience of therapy. On the other hand, their experience may raise a much larger issue, the fundamental need to grow as a whole person and to confront other ways their growth has been blocked. Some clients will not get the changes they need in brief therapy and will choose to invest more of themselves in pursuing the bigger issue. At that point the therapeutic contract is renegotiated for the next phase, which we call the deepening phase.

THE DEEPENING PHASE

This phase of therapy differs from the initial phase in several respects. Primarily there is a shift in emphasis from problem-solving or symptom-focused brief intervention to more broad-based change and growth. The therapeutic contract in this phase, while still firmly grounded in the client's original request for therapy, now is renegotiated for more fundamental change and personal growth. The therapist's perspective plays a stronger role in the therapeutic contract at this time, pointing the way to what might be required for further work. However, it is important in the renegotiation of the therapeutic contract that the therapist avoid taking responsibility for the client's goals. The therapeutic process is more effective when we make the contract quite explicit and clearly leave the energy and motivation for therapy with the client.

While in the initial phase the family members' denial or lack of awareness might have been ignored or dealt with only minimally, in this phase confronting and facing denial is a central part of the work. Now clients need to examine many of the subtler aspects of their self-destructive or abusive behavior, identify the sources of traumatic and inherited shame, and take down the walls between their affect and their history. Most importantly, family members begin the long-term process of becoming self-affirming persons.

Substantial long-term dependencies and addictions, the shame-maintaining behaviors, do not change quickly. Sometimes with new insight or effective support a person is able to step off the shame-bound cycle and let go of an obsessive or compulsive pattern quite abruptly. This can happen in the initial phase and may be the bridge into the deepening phase. While this sudden reform looks like improvement and is very encouraging, such a dramatic event by no means signals permanent change. In fact, it leaves a person and the whole family in a very unstable position. The most likely outcome is that they will return in a short while to the previous pattern, unless intensive therapy and support are provided for the gradual integration of new interactional patterns.

Once clients step out of the control-release-dominated, shame-bound cycle, their central way of controlling and organizing feelings has been removed. At this point people are in a position emotionally and developmentally similar to adolescence, i.e, flooded with feelings but with little in the way of personal experience and resources for dealing with them. The old compulsive pattern which maintained the shame, covered the feelings, and stabilized the system has been suspended. New learning about how to be a person has not yet occurred. This is when systemic change can begin. The rigid and resistant patterns give way to meaningful therapy because the insulation or anesthesia provided by the dependency has been suspended. Now a contract for long-term work is indicated and now is the time for the therapist to promise to remain available for the hard work ahead.

CLIENT: I feel so scared to try to exist without ever being able to turn to alcohol for some relief.

THERAPIST: I'm not surprised that you're afraid. In a sense it's been your only reliable friend. Now you will begin to feel much more vulnerable and have many feelings that have been covered over. Your therapy here involves learning to have real friends and exist with your feelings. That will take some time and will be painful at times. But as long as you are willing to work at it, I will hang in here with you.

Normally, in the course of the deepening phase, one member of the system makes a move toward more mature, healthy functioning before the others. The repercussions can be chaotic. The therapist needs to have a compass in this process, in the form of a systemic understanding, because it can be very tempting to become judgmental or see what's happening only in individual terms.

One area for change is a marital relationship in which both spouses are locked in a power struggle. Finally one of them stops playing the control "game" and focuses on her or his own personal development. Another case involves a family in which one member is blatantly acting out in self-indulgent and or abusive ways. This person gets confronted effectively with his or her behavior and gives it up as part of the therapy. What usually follows is that the complementarity of the relationship becomes highlighted. The subtler side of the spouse's or other family members' behavior becomes more blatant.

In one instance a couple in therapy was focused on the addictive spending of the husband. He was clearly outrageous in his spending behavior, which he staunchly justified and explained for several weeks. When he acknowledged that he might need to do something different about his spending, he agreed to temporarily stop all use of money except for food and transportation, until he could begin to develop a more reasonable pattern. What emerged next was the wife's pattern of denigrating and blaming him for almost anything that happened in her life. This patten had previously been safely covered by the husband's more blatant behavior. Now that he ended *his* behavior, *hers* became more extreme. Now he felt stronger about himself and could challenge her on her part.

In other situations where the fusion and enmeshment are extreme, when one of the family members begins to respond in more self-responsible, individuated ways, other family members are likely to react as if they'd been betrayed or treated very unfairly. Blatantly or subtly, they will demand that the person return to previous patterns. Complementarity is also seen when one family member seems to be acting out the discomfort of another. For example, children may act out the unacknowledged anxiety of a parent or the unacknowledged conflict in a parental relationship. Or, one spouse may scapegoat himself or herself in response to the nonverbalized or implied discomfort of the other.

What we see in this pattern is such a fusion of personal boundaries and such a protectionist system that a member acts out as a way to protect himself and others from anxiety. The acting-out takes endless forms. The person may say something so outrageous that it draws everyone's anger to her or him, or become physically ill, or get drunk. When the person who is acting out seems to end up in a one-down position, the therapist can ask a question that gets at the system, for example, "Who are you protecting by this behavior?" Or, "What do you think your husband was feeling just before you started to act that way?" "Do you do this for him?"

Just as the immaturity of one family member supports the immaturity of another, growth and change of one stimulate growth on the part of another. The system changes as the individuals change their behavior, and that occurs in spurts and starts, in a back and forth process.

Therapy in this phase often involves identifying and teaching the difference between anger and abuse. Seldom are members of the shame-bound family able to make this distinction. When they themselves get angry or someone else does, it immediately feels dangerous, abusive, or out of control. The therapist can coach people how to be open and direct in expression of anger without being disrespectful or assaultive.

Movement into the intimate quadrant of family interaction calls for expression of "hot" feelings of many kinds. (See Figure 7, Chapter 6.) We often see families who have moved beyond the active abuse in their history but are now so controlled that they are stuck in the calm quadrant. As a result their relationships are boring or dead and no differences can be resolved. Sometimes we help people find their angry feelings by going through the motions of being angry and seeing how it feels. To help them make this affective contact and further accept the feelings, we may suggest that they hit pillows with their hands or pound with soft-material bats while loudly yelling. "I am angry at you" may be a clear, respectful message. "I am angry at you because you always make me so tense" is a blaming and potentially assaultive message.

As people progress in therapy, as they deepen in their relationships to themselves and to others, they find themselves feeling vulnerable. Because of their shame background, this experience will feel like something is wrong. It has been when they were vulnerable that they were abused. Vulnerable feelings have become paired with shame. What they can learn through the therapists's coaching is that vulnerability is what makes it possible to become genuinely close to another person. A therapist can give some simple reassurance that its all right to feel.

CLIENT: I feel so awful telling you these things about myself. You must be sitting there thinking I'm a terrible person.
THERAPIST: What I really feel is a deep sense of respect for your courage. It takes great courage to look at what you've been seeing and I respect you for sticking with it.

When family members become disrespectful of one another in the session, the therapist may be the person who has the awareness to point it out. Often both the aggressor and the victim of an abusive exchange are unaware that it has happened. In this way the family session is a learning laboratory.

CLIENT: (to another family member) If you didn't have such a weird looking face maybe it would be easier to listen to you.

THERAPIST: Hold it right there! That kind of talk is really abusive and we can't have it. What happened with you that brought out this reaction?

CLIENT: Well, she was telling me I never listen to her but I try. She just doesn't realize how much I try to listen to her.

THERAPIST: Did you have some feeling when you heard her say this?

CLIENT: Yeah! I felt bad!

THERAPIST: So you felt bad and then struck out at her?

CLIENT: Um hmm.

THERAPIST: I can understand your feeling bad when she said that, but you can't get mean with your words when you feel bad. I think she deserves an apology from you. Then let's talk some more about those bad feelings you had.

Comment: In addition to the identification of abusive language in the above dialogue, the therapist was coaching the movement from a shame response to a guilt response. When the client acknowledged his behavior and became accountable, he could feel some guilt and make repair, a self-esteem-lifting, rather than a shaming, experience.

After much of the work described above has been completed, after the family members have moved through denial about their own shame and its origins, it is often useful to bring in the siblings and parents of the adult members of the family (Framo 1976). This is done with considerable advance planning and preparation, especially since these family members often live at great distances. These sessions are often dramatic events because the siblings and parents are clearly coming to be of help to their loved one in therapy. This is a time when the family history is discussed, old abuses uncovered, emotional cut-offs ended, and new relationships begun.

When people travel from out of town for these sessions, we generally arrange two extended sessions on two consecutive days. On the first day we meet for three hours; that is generally an opening up time, under the leadership of the client. He or she will have an agenda which has been formulated with the therapist in the weeks before this session. The therapist needs to keep two principles clearly in mind. First is that these family members do not have a therapeutic contract. They have come in the interest of their loved one, and it would be inappropriate to try to do therapy or change them. Second, the family is not to blame and should not be "ambushed" for all the personal misery the client has experienced. When family members come they often expect to be blamed and are either on guard or prepared to confess. We hold that the most helpful thing they can do is to be as honest as they can be, suspend some of the traditional rules they've had about what can be talked about, and trust that discussion among them will be healing. Simply sharing information can be explosive in some instances, a profound relief in many — but rarely has it not been very helpful.

Usually a two-hour session is scheduled for the second day. By that time people have had a night to think about the previous meeting and begin to react to it. Sometimes more things get opened up in this session, building upon the previous one. It must be said, too, that in some instances the therapeutic experience for the client involves finding how fixed, how toxic, and how unavailable the family system is.

In this deepening phase the therapist is a coach for the creative process of becoming a real person and developing a relationship with oneself. Many methods can be used. We sometimes use daily or periodic journal writing, asking clients, in their own privacy, to make notes about their experiences, feelings, doubts and questions, and to reflect upon their own process. While the privacy of one's journal and authority over one's own personal boundaries are extremely important in this process, the client may choose to share some parts of the journal with other family members or the therapist.

Other "homework" is used to lower the walls between one's

history and one's affect. For instance, we sometimes ask clients to visit the grave of a dead parent, sibling or friend. We suggest to them that they talk out loud to the dead person about pertinent issues in their relationship. This usually is about old matters that were never resolved, but it can also be about recent events that somehow intersect the relationship with the dead person. Paraphrasing the opening line from the movie *I Never Sang For My Father*: Death ends a life, it does not end a relationship. Reopening the reality of the relationship can be painful – as well as revitalizing and freeing.

In the same spirit we encourage people to bring old photographs to the session. They are used both to communicate a more tangible sense of the past to the therapist and to help clients recontact their own past and family history, thereby gaining a feeling of continuity.

Recording dreams and bringing them to the session can be a useful way to develop a more solid reference to oneself. Becoming acquainted with the world of one's dreams does not require that one develop a sophisticated knowledge of symbols and interpretation. Just sharing dreams and talking about this "journey that I went on beyond my conscious control" can serve a useful function. The daily practice of meditation, relaxation, or physical exercise serve similar self-affirming purposes.

As our colleague Rene Schwartz says, many people emerging from a shame-bound system "don't know how to use discovery for growth." Anything can be used for shame and usually is in this system. Since much of the deepening phase is about getting beyond denial, discovering history and uncovering reality, there is ample material for a shameful person to use against himself. The therapist must help the client reframe learning so that it is available for growth rather than defeat. We do not promote a "Pollyanna" view of the world in our reframing, but we try to block the negativistic, self-defeating shame response.

CLIENT: I feel so terrible about myself this week. Ever since
　　　I realized, last time we met, how much my parents were

emotionally absent from me as a child, I have just wanted to hide my face when I am with anyone.

THERAPIST: It sounds like, as you uncovered that old situation, you also reactivated your old feelings of shame about being treated that way.

CLIENT: I don't know, but I don't feel like I can tell anybody about it.

THERAPIST: Can you picture that small child that you were, sitting next to you here now?

CLIENT: I suppose.

THERAPIST: Could you be a friend to that little girl? Maybe even put your arm around her?

CLIENT: That's what I would like.

THERAPIST: I'd like you to bring her to mind from time to time over the next few days. Practice being friendly and warm with her. Don't judge her. Just take her the way she is.

Throughout the process of therapy with shame-bound families strong emphasis is placed on a systems perspective at several levels. This has taught us as therapists to see ourselves and our families as part of a larger system that has healing powers. The first level of systems thinking is the individual. The second level, that of the nuclear family, is the major subject of this book. The third level, the affiliative family network outside the biological family, is extremely important. No therapy experience alone is sufficient to provide all that is needed in the recovery process. Characteristically, many of the people we work with do not have a very well developed friendship network.

As part of their recovery, clients are encouraged, coached and referred to make affiliations outside. On many occasions the referral is to a therapy group, other times it is to a class or workshop. We encourage participation in community organizations, church, synagogue, and social groups which have a humanizing atmosphere. A crucial part of this work is referral of alcoholic and addicted clients and family members to Alcoholics Anonymous, Al-Anon, or parallel groups using the same 12-step program of recovery, such as Overeaters Anony-

mous, O-Anon, Sex Addicts Anonymous, Co-Sex Addicts
Anonymous, Spenders Anonymous, Bulimics Anonymous,
etc. These self-help groups provide affiliation with fellow
sufferers and an aspect of recovery that is not provided in
therapy.

Many times the family therapist becomes the coordinator
of several therapeutic endeavors involving different family
members. No single therapist is enough. We mobilize the
power of a system to treat the family system. A couple of
family members may be in group therapy with other therapists, and a third may be in individual therapy with someone
else. All the while the family therapist is maintaining the
family perspective, acting as the generalist, maintaining contact with the various therapists and coordinating the work.
In instances of alcoholism or advanced stages of addiction,
it is often our practice to refer the family for specialized treatment for the addiction and then pick up on the deepening
phase after that has been completed.

A fourth system is that of the therapist's professional and
personal colleagues, many of whom are working with parts
of the same families. In order for therapists to maintain appropriate therapeutic boundaries, they need to be part of
their own system. They need to have an ongoing professional
system of support, consultation, and reality orientation, with
its own regenerative processes. Many of these families are extremely difficult to work with. They are stressful and abusive
not only for their members but also for the therapist, who,
as a human being, is not at all immune to the destructive
process.

We speak of ourselves as a system of therapists doing
therapy with systems. While a therapist may be in a family
session without the benefit of a co-therapist, the fact that a
closely working network of therapists knows his or her work
with this family and also knows the major outlines of his or
her personal life makes the boundary between family and
therapist more secure. It is important to make use of co-
therapists when needed, bring in a consultant for a one-time
evaluation, or call on a specialist to evaluate for chemical or
other addictions when that is indicated.

The therapist working with these systems needs to have a well-developed awareness of her or his own shame, addiction, boundary and control issues, both personally and in the larger family system. One needs to have an awareness of one's personal tendency to overreact emotionally to the heavily laden and provocative stories and interactions which unfold in the therapy room. One needs to have a well developed ability to take a stand or set clear limits with one's clients, and yet not be self-righteous about it. We have seen repeatedly, in our own development and in our colleagues', that if a therapist has not faced those issues personally, chances are that she or he will enable the clients to avoid them. Facing them personally instills a healthy humility in us as therapists and increases our authentic professional strength.

THE CLOSING PHASE

Coming to the end of therapy after a successful passage through the deepening phase is a profound moment. It is triumphal; it is affirming of the human spirit to confront great problems and not only survive but grow and become stronger. In that way our work brings us wonderful, inspiring, real-life adventures every day. This is not to say that everyone reaches this stage. Even those who decide to enter the deepening phase sometimes lose the motivation to carry on, or lose trust in themselves or their therapist to do what needs to be done here. Nor are we claiming anything like a "cure." What people have by this stage of the work is a system in which to live, a network of support outside their immediate family, and a personal sense of dignity and accountability for themselves and their recovery.

The relationship between family members and therapist has grown over the months or even years that this therapy has progressed. By this time, not only does the therapist know intimately the lives of the clients, but they also know a great deal about their therapist. The relationship started with much more form and strategy than substance and trust. It ends with the fullness and substance that comes from knowing each other. Clients may not know the details of their therapist's personal life but they know his or her responses to life, they know the subtleties and nuances of how he or she responds. They have come to know their therapist as a person. The relationship now is based on honest exchange as persons, with the clients having gradually taken more responsibility for their own direction and growth.

When this stage is reached, it is time to end. The ending takes place planfully, paying respect to the significance of the journey that has been taken together. Many times this journey has been life-saving both literally and spiritually.

For the client this ending is a kind of emancipation from the foster-parent therapist. As such it is not absolute. Just as the emancipating adolescent is strengthened by returning home for support from time to time, the client needs to know that the door to the therapy room is not locked. We develop long-term consultant relationships with many families who might return after several years for help in a transition stage or reinforcement in a crisis or assistance with another facet of work.

When the last session comes according to the plan made by clients and therapist, we often reminisce about the journey. We talk about what were some of the meaningful moments, the doubts we had about each other at given times, and the crises that were precipitated by therapy and lived through. In this process the progress is affirmed, not as an absolute but as a resource, a roadmap, a set of tools for becoming what we are – truly human.

Reference

Framo, J. (1976). Family of origin as therapeutic resource for adults in marital and family therapy. *Family Process, 15*, 193–210.

INDEX

187